Elian: Shame or Sham?

Elian: Shame or Sham?

Cesar Guerra

Writers Club Press

San Jose New York Lincoln Shanghai

Elian: Shame or Sham?

Writers Club Press
an imprint of iUniverse, Inc.

For information address:
iUniverse, Inc.
5220 S. 16th St., Suite 200
Lincoln, NE 68512
www.iuniverse.com

ISBN: 0-595-23772-X

Printed in the United States of America

To my wife, who encouraged me to finish writing this book. I could not have done that without her unending support and help.

To my children, earth angels each one; and to my friends who want to know my opinion even if we don't always agree.

Contents

INTRODUCTION

The purpose of this book is to describe and analyze a tragic event that happened in the closing months of 1999 and early part of the new millennium as it was reported by the national and local news media. This incident caught the public's attention throughout the United States and with great possibility a large portion of the civilized world.

I am referring to the rescue and subsequent saga of a young Cuban-born child and his dramatic and relatively short stay in the United States of America. The most creative writer in the movie industry couldn't have come up with a better plot, more dramatic and profound emotional results than this modern-day sad and real life soap opera: The Elian Gonzalez case.

Elian was just five years old when he was rescued by two American fishermen far off shore, in the deep waters of the Gulfstream between the Bahamas and the southeastern tip of the peninsula of Florida.

When found, the boat-wrecked boy informed his rescuers he had been holding onto an inner tube for two days and that he had just lost his mother Elizabeth Brotons who had drowned in front of him. His mother, her boyfriend, Elian and eleven other Cubans were attempting to flee the communist regime of Fidel Castro in a 16-foot boat powered with an outboard motor.

On a daily basis for almost six months we heard the news reporters discussing the Elian Gonzalez case and they informed the public immediately of the surprisingly quick decision taken by the INS (Immigration and Naturalization Service) to release him to his father's uncle, Elian's great-uncle Lazaro Gonzalez who was living with his family in the Little Havana section of Miami. The great-uncle's daughter Marisleysis, the little boy's second cousin, soon became Elian's surrogate mother.

1

Other than considering it a contemporary divine miracle as it was widely described by all the reporters after interviewing the rescuers, the survival of Elian itself does raise some questions, as do some of the subsequent events that followed. Many of those events do not have any logical explanation.

I must state very firmly from the beginning of this writing that I will not try to force my opinion on you regarding any particular situation as described in this book.

I will cite some of my findings or my own experiences in similar or likely circumstances, and from time to time when appropriate, I will include excerpts or full statements and news releases from the INS and the Justice Department of the United States. I want to mention that some of those excerpts are from articles of several journalists and reporters from the news media.

I want to emphasize that it is my honest intention to just give you, the reader, an opportunity to reach your own conclusions while you follow the dramatic events as presented to the public.

Was this tragic event a true survival story of a miracle boy? Or was this a premeditated and extremely well executed plan developed by powerful forces with enough resources to carry out this operation successfully?

Every coin has two sides. The imprint on each side represents something symbolic and meaningful for the issuing country. As presented to the general public this case definitely has two sides like a coin, and the circumstances as it developed definitely has two faces or imprints. In this case unfortunately neither side of the coin is attractive.

Many lives were touched and affected by this tragedy and only time may finally disclose the naked truth of this episode.

While I was still gathering information, researching and taking the necessary notes to start the manuscript of this book, I talked to a good friend of mine regarding my intention to write about the Elian Gonzalez affair. I knew that this subject was very close to her heart. She and her husband were among the thousands of very young girls and boys that were spirited from Cuba to the United States in the early 60's through a Cuban children's program called Operation Peter Pan.

She told me that she went all the way to 'Little Havana' to offer her moral support to Lazaro Gonzalez and his family in their effort to keep Elian in the United States. In her sensible and humoristic way she told me, "I wish you good luck! My friend, you will need to become a modern-day Sherlock Holmes to find out the truth about this case." Her comments didn't surprise me but only further enticed me to continue with this work. I will never pretend to be Mr. Holmes but in many opportunities I would like to use his famous line, "Elementary, Dr. Watson, elementary."

Sadly my writing may hurt the feelings of some people involved or sympathetic with the idea of keeping the young boy in the land of the free and the home of the brave.

It is possible I might not ever find out the truth about the Elian quandary and the questions raised within these pages will go ignored, but it is my hope that the reader will think twice about the Elian Gonzalez saga and how it was handled. Was it a Shame or a Sham?

1

PRELUDE TO A DISASTER

November 22nd, 1963 is remembered as a dreadful day in the history of the United States of America. The assassination of President John F. Kennedy will always be known as a poignant time in the history of America. Was it a bad omen to start an escape journey from Cuba to the United States on the 36th anniversary of such a tragic event? As we were informed through the news media this ill-fated trip had its own frightful and fatal ending for eleven adults and culminated in one of the most volatized child custody cases in recent history.

The American public learned that on November 22, 1999 Elian, his mother Elizabeth, her boyfriend, and eleven other Cubans had left their island aboard a 16-foot boat powered by an outboard motor in an attempt to reach the United States. It was the beginning of a string of events that might add another black dot to every twenty-second day in the month of November.

As I mentioned in the Introduction section of this book, I have numerous questions and I cannot find a logical explanation to many of them. For example, this little boy was only five years old when all these distressing events developed in front of his tender young eyes and, as we learned later on, he did not speak English when he was pulled from the Gulfstream waters. Did his rescuers converse in Spanish? When and how did the American authorities and the news media learn about the exact date of the beginning of this evidently ill planned voyage? Was it Elian who told the story about the trip? Otherwise how did the authorities learn of the details?

I wonder what physical condition the boy was in when he was hauled from the ocean, taking into consideration that he was floating in an auto inner tube for two consecutive days and nights. Was Elian in shock or traumatized by witnessing the drowning of his mother? We were told that he and his mother both held onto the same inner tube.

Maybe this information reached our authorities and media through the other two survivors of the capsized boat after they reached Florida's shores by their own efforts…Evidently they had another inner tube and got separated in the Gulfstream waters from Elian and his mother. Then, how and when did they learn about Elizabeth's fate?

By now we all have seen, at one time or another, pictures of the most rudimentary rafts that lay in the compounds of some of the United States Coast Guard bases in the southern areas of the State of Florida, after they had carried very desperate Cubans to some of the small pieces of land known as the Florida Keys.

Their courage, audacity and complete disregard of safety are remarkable and sometimes almost unbelievable. But everyone would agree that desperate people do desperate and unwise things and this could be one of those cases. Without touching upon the political aspects that pushed them to take such daring risks, it should be recognized that most of the successful journeys could be categorized as miraculous feats.

Unfortunately not all of the fleeing Cubans succeeded in reaching their dreamland and freedom on the shores of the United States. Many uncounted lives have been lost in the waters of the Gulfstream, in the open seas. Probably many more will die attempting to leave behind the horrors and pains imposed on them by the communist authorities in control of the suffered and tyrannized Cuban nation.

Without imposing my personal opinions I'll try to describe the 'open water' capabilities of a '16-foot motorboat.' Some may disagree with me, but I would not myself venture out into the deep waters of the Gulfstream in a 16-footer during the winter months, and I have been involved in boating and sailing more years than I care to remember.

The following description is to help readers not familiar with boating to know the configuration and capacity of such a vessel. On average, the width of a 16-foot boat is about 1/3 of its length; in other words, between 5 and 6 feet at the widest part and only in some special or odd designs it has more than 2-1/2 to 3 feet of freeboard. (Freeboard is the distance between the waterline and the top of the side of the boat.)

Normally this type of boat has a capacity for four passengers including the skipper and it would be considered safe enough for short, close to shore excursions. Six adults riding aboard a boat that size is not very wise, but it would not probably endanger them in calm and moderate inland waters. It likely would not tip over or put their lives at risk.

Thirteen adults and one child aboard a 16-footer? That's almost incredible! They had to be actually sitting on top of each other. Thirteen adults alone would be almost 2000 pounds in the boat considering an average weight of 150 pounds per passenger. A 16-foot boat by today's safety standards has a maximum weight capacity of 1300 pounds. Besides the passenger weight, one must also take into consideration the weight of supplies including drinking water, the outboard motor and the necessary fuel to reach the keys or mainland across the Gulfstream! Passenger and supply weight certainly put that boat at a dangerous over maximum capacity weight situation.

I'm curious to know how they carried the two tire-sized inner tubes that ultimately saved Elian and two other passengers.

I am sure we all will agree that in the rush and desperation to leave Cuba the sense of safety of Lazaro Rafael Munero, supposedly the person in charge of the boat, and as a matter of fact all of the adults in that vessel, seemed to be thrown overboard right before they departed. The results: eleven adult lives lost with indelible and disturbing impact into the lives of thousands and thousands more, who in one way or another were affected by this tragedy.

Again, the media reported that they had learned that this was the second departure of the 'Elian boat.' It was reported that they had attempted to leave Cuba a few days prior to November 22nd but had to return to Cuban shores because of mechanical problems with the outboard motor.

Two big questions come to my mind: Was this a sanctioned official trip approved by the communist Cuban government? How and when did the Cuban government learn that Lazaro Rafael Munero, Elizabeth's alleged boyfriend, was in charge of the boat? They further accused him of intimidating Elizabeth to leave Cuba. Did Lazaro Rafael also intimidate the other eleven passengers to get aboard his boat?

It must be emphatically stated that when you try to escape from the totalitarian regime in control of Cuba you do it with the most strict secrecy, and more likely in the stealth of the night! The Cuban coast guards regularly patrol their shores by water and land, and the civilian/militia members of the local CDR (Committee for the Defense of the Revolution) keep a very close watch on every move made by the citizens living in the area under their control. Those 'comrades' are extremely unfriendly to anyone trying to leave Cuba by any means or under any circumstances.

I'm wondering…Did all of the passengers stay aboard the boat while Lazaro Rafael secured the spare parts or while he found a mechanic to make the repairs to the outboard motor? When did all that happen…in broad daylight or was it under the darkness of night? It would be astonishing to learn that all the passengers went home, and a few days later they gathered together to again board the same boat while avoiding detection one more time from the communist Cuban authorities. It would be very interesting to know through who or how our media learned about all these misfortunes.

Provided you have found a satisfactory answer to some or any of the above questions, we learned that the second departure took the escaping conspirators and their motorboat to a point of no return.

I must assume that Lazaro Rafael Munero, the acting skipper, knew how to operate his boat and was aware of its capabilities (speed and distance it could safely cover) even as overloaded as this one supposedly was. At best I can hope that he had an idea about where he was going.

The following explanation is to give readers not familiar with the crossing from Cuba to Florida an idea of the risk the passengers of that fateful boat took on that 22nd of November in 1999.

It is general knowledge that Cuba is only 90 miles away from the United States. To determine this distance it needs to be calculated from Key West on the U.S. side and a point between the bays of Matanzas and Cardenas, in Matanzas Province in Cuba. It must be noted that traveling by road, which is almost a straight line, the distance from Key West to Miami on the south tip of the peninsula of Florida is about 160 miles.

It would be a fairly good guess that the departure of "Elian's boat" was from any spot between the Bay of Cardenas, (the city were he and his parents lived) and the beach-resort area called Varadero, approximately 20 miles further east along the north Cuban coast. The shoreline westward from that point on is too rough to launch and take aboard passengers on a small boat. I might be wrong by a few miles when I quote these distances so please accept my apologies. It has been about 40 years since I last handled a navigation chart of that area.

For the sake of comparison a similar crossing in a well equipped, safe power yacht traveling at about 25 knots would take approximately 4 hours to travel the distance between Cuba and Key West, if the weather is good and the Gulfstream waters are calm.

A 16-foot outboard powered boat grossly over its maximum capacity could not make more than 4 to 5 knots safely and is not by any stretch of the imagination the proper vessel for this crossing. Many times I saw 8 to 10 foot waves while sailing across those same waters aboard a 67-foot racing sailboat.

Recently I saw a brochure from a state of the art American boat manufacturer wherein they pictured a boat of the same size, with five male adults standing in the boat's deck close to the side to show its stability. The boat was tilted by the weight of the persons aboard and the freeboard was only about eight inches above the water line.

Can you imagine thirteen adults and one child, two full size inner tubes plus provisions crowded into a sixteen-foot boat? No wonder it was reported that the Cubans' boat capsized in the Gulfstream waters the next day, November 23, 1999. It would be interesting to know if they even reached the Gulfstream itself, running approximately four to five nautical miles off the northwestern shores of Cuba.

Now, how do we know with any certain degree of assurance the veracity of this happening, the exact day of the sinking and the complete disappearance of the boat? To my knowledge no debris or wreckage of that boat was ever found. At the time the boat 'capsized' it would not have yet been within the boundaries of the Bermuda Triangle.

A voluntary organization named Brothers to the Rescue out of Miami make almost daily flights over the Florida Straits. Their gallant pilot-members fly between Florida, Cuba and the Bahamas to help spot Cuban rafters or boats that capsized and tossed its occupants to the waters of the Gulfstream. When the pilots spot a raft or boat in distress they drop drinking water and other supplies, and they have a tough decision to make instantly. If the pilots alert the U.S. Coast Guard about the Cubans, they are intercepted before they reach United States soil and are returned to Cuba immediately. But if the Cubans persist in their intentions to reach the U.S. at any risk, the pilots don't interfere with them, and the fleeing refugees may reach American soil, or die at sea.

On February 24, 1996 two of the Brothers to the Rescue planes were shot down by fighter jets of the Cuban Air Force and four members of that organization, Armando Alejandre, Jr., Carlos Costa, Pablo Morales and Mario de la Pena lost their lives as a result of that attack while they were performing their humanitarian efforts. The Cuban community in exile will always remember those unheralded heroes.

The United States policy regarding Cubans attempting to reach the U.S. by boat, raft or any floating device was changed by an agreement reached between the Clinton Administration and Castro's communist government. The Cuban Adjustment Act of 1966 was changed or amended in 1994, allowing for the immigration process to be initiated only for those who touch U.S. soil. The ones caught off shore or rescued from the ocean are returned to Cuba, unless their physical condition warrants for them to be rushed to an American hospital as a humanitarian action.

The intention of this book is not to analyze in depth the political situation in Cuba, but have you ever wondered what is the fate of those delivered back to the 'comrades'?

There is no record of the pilots of Brothers to the Rescue reporting any boat, wreckage or survivors floating in the Gulfstream from November 22nd through the 25th.

What do we know about the other ten passengers? How did the authorities and the press in United States learn about their fate? When did they die? These questions have gone unanswered because they were never asked.

It has been reported by our media that on November 25, 1999 two passengers of the sunken boat floated ashore and touched American land and they were whisked away by the authorities to an INS processing center in South Miami. Who and where are they now? Was any reporter able to locate and interview them? Not a single word about their whereabouts!

However, the television news media gave us immediate information that on the same day cousins Donato Dalrymple and Sam Ciancio were fishing way off shore in the Gulfstream and had rescued a little boy clinging for life from an inner tube. How did Donato and Sam communicate with Elian? Did they speak Spanish? That episode of this drama will be analyzed in the next chapter.

Before we go forward I want to recap some of the previous questions. Assuming the whole story is true, who knows what really happened aboard the ill-fated boat before the sinking? Who told the media about the first failed departure and the exact day of the second attempt?

When and how did they learn about the size of the boat in question? Was it a wood, aluminum or fiberglass hull?

I know that almost all old Cuban boat hulls were made of hard wood, and with great buoyancy. I don't recall many aluminum boats back there. Was this a modern fiberglass boat? I would like to assume that even the most backward and low cost builder in Cuba would install some foam flotation materials under the floor, foredeck and seats to prevent the boat from sinking, even if it were to be flooded!

When and under what circumstances did the other passengers drown and die?

Does anyone know the answer to these questions with any degree of certainty? So far the only information we have of this trip are the recollections of Elian.

I will not share my answers to any of these questions. It is entirely up to you to reach your own conclusions.

2

RESCUE FROM THE GULFSTREAM

'Elian's boat' left Cuba on November 22, 1999 and it capsized the next day, November 23rd. Further reports describe how Elian was found drifting in the Gulfstream on November 25th, the same day two other Cuban survivors from the same boat came ashore, landing between Miami Beach and Fort Lauderdale. This piece of the puzzle also requires an analysis.

As described in the previous chapter, I don't know of anyone reporting the time when the Cuban boat and its passengers finally ventured out in its attempt to reach the United States. If I knew the time of departure I could approximately estimate the place of the capsizing and disappearance of the boat and when all of the passengers went floating in the Gulfstream. Unfortunately there is no such record, and the only persons that could answer that question are unreachable. Elian is back in Cuba and the two other two survivors vanished into thin air.

It is not my intention to speculate or try to reconstruct the sad and traumatic moments when the other ten passengers drowned; but, as we learned, only three adults and a child survived floating and clinging from inner tubes for two days, without any food, drinking water or protection from the weather. We might need to add one additional day to their depravations; the time they were aboard the boat before it capsized.

Accepting as fact the crowdedness on the boat in which they were trying to leave Cuba, it is a smart guess that it sunk shortly after entering the Gulfstream.

A question in this regard: Did the three adults and child holding onto the inner tubes drift for approximately 200 miles in two days? Even if the distance they drifted is shorter than that, it is difficult to believe they could travel that far without drinking water or food. They were constantly exposed to the elements, not counting the ocean predators that lurk in those waters looking for food.

Elian was on the front page of many newspapers and in the evening news of the major TV networks as soon as he was in the hands of the United States Coast Guard and reached land. He was retrieved from the fishermen's boat after they notified the authorities by radio about their finding in the Gulfstream. Who informed the news media about the little boy's rescue? The reporters and photographers were waiting for him upon his arrival to the hospital!

Elian's arrival to the hospital was photographed and featured on the front-page of the newspapers and on the TV news. The pictures and video I saw of Elian when he was rushed into the emergency room of Memorial Hospital in Hollywood, Florida, showed an expressionless scared child strapped to a stretcher. But I didn't see any signs of sunburn, blisters nor swollen eyelids or lips. True symptoms of dehydration and hypothermia may not show up in a photo, but are very likely to be suffered by anyone from exposure to the ocean's salt water and weather for a long period of time.

That brings me to another question I try to understand. Why was Elian not taken to Jackson Memorial Hospital in Miami? He didn't speak English when he was rescued and that hospital in Miami has many on their staff that could communicate easily with the young Cuban patient in his native and only language, Spanish.

I have nothing but the highest respect for the medical doctors, nurses and other assistants of Memorial Hospital in Hollywood, Florida. I lived in that charming city for 21 years and I had many opportunities to visit the hospital and I used its facilities myself on an occasion or two. I couldn't commend them enough for their kindness, expertise and professionalism.

However, it can be easily guessed that you would find more Spanish speaking physicians and staff in Miami than in Hollywood and verbal communications between patient and doctor are vital in emergency cases.

Anyway, the final results of the treatment given to Elian could not be any better. He was discharged from the Hollywood facility the very next day after being admitted as an emergency room patient. Evidently the doctor in charge considered the child in good enough health to be released to the Immigration and Naturalization Service agents overseeing Elian's case.

Many lives are saved daily with or without any medical or physiological explanation and I certainly believe in miracles. But, two days and nights floating in the ocean definitely would have left some physical marks, signs or evidence that could be noted at simple sight.

The supervisor of the Medical Records department and the administrator of Memorial Hospital in Hollywood will certainly deny access to Elian's file of the examination and the physical condition reports of Elian Gonzalez when he was admitted to and when he was released from the hospital. Obviously they have an obligation to protect the privacy and confidentiality between doctors and patient. Only a court order for an official hearing would release the hospital and doctors from that responsibility. Still, it would be very interesting to see those records.

You may be able to review the above-mentioned picture in the archives of some newspapers in your area. Ask to see their publication dated November 26th or 27th of 1999. It will likely have Elian's picture in it. The public library in your area should have a collection of old newspapers and if so, you can ask to see the copy for those dates.

By the way, what physical condition were the two Cuban adult survivors in when taken into custody by the INS? Did they receive any medical assistance or were they sent directly to the processing center in South Miami? Nobody knows...I have not seen any published photographs of them.

As a hobby for many years I participated in outdoor sports, mainly boating and sailing. Very often I sailed across the Gulfstream from Havana to the Dry Tortugas bank located 60 miles west of Key West. I am very blessed to remain in good physical condition and health. Thanks to the area were I live my skin is fairly well tanned all year around. With that short explanation I want to share with you a simple and almost silly test I did on myself.

I decided to hold onto an inflatable plastic lounge while floating in a screened enclosed swimming pool. I wanted to know how my body would react and for how long I could go without drinking or eating while holding onto the float. Of course, I knew the circumstances were much different than floating offshore because I could stop the test at any time I wanted to and my life was not at all at risk.

During the winter months the Gulfstream water temperature averages between low and mid seventies degrees. Sometimes even lower if it is affected by a cold front typical during those months. A prolonged immersion in those waters would cause some loss of body temperature (hypothermia), but the water in the swimming pool I was in registered 87 degrees. The pool's filter pump was running to keep the water circulating, forcing me to steadily move my legs to remain in the deep end since I didn't want to touch the bottom of the pool. I was wearing sunglasses and had my cap on.

After a little over an hour of floating in the water I noticed that my fingers were wrinkled like ripe prunes and my arms started feeling the effects of the effort of holding onto the float. My lower body began to feel stiff. When mild cramps started taking hold of my right leg I knew it was time to quit the test.

I was not extremely sunburned, but my back felt the effects of the sunrays filtering through the screen above the pool. I was not really that thirsty because I cheated somewhat when I splashed some of the pool's water on my face wetting my lips.

Yes, I accept the fact that I am not as strong as I used to be. Yes, I know that in my subconscious I knew that I was not fighting for survival and I could get out of the pool at any time I wanted to. How long could I hold on if I knew that I depended on my strength to save my life? I really don't know.

But I am sure that my fingers, hands, arms, toes, feet, legs and the rest of my entire body would show the results of overexposure to the ocean's salt water and the elements.

I was very thankful I was not in the rough waters of the Gulfstream but in a fresh water swimming pool.

3

ELIAN RELEASED FROM HOSPITAL

On November 26, 1999, the day after he was rescued from the Gulfstream, Elian was evidently in such good physical condition that the doctor in charge of his medical needs determined that he could be released from the hospital.

While in the hospital, did the little boy mention to the INS agents that his father, in Cuba, had an uncle living in the United States? How did Lazaro Gonzalez and his family learn of the boy's dramatic arrival to Hollywood, Florida? Did they learn it through the news? It is very possible.

Otherwise, the Miami office of the Immigration and Naturalization Service must have worked very hard to find, in one day, Elian's distant family relatives living in the northwest area of Miami, about 20 miles south of Hollywood.

Gonzalez is a very common surname among the Hispanic population living in South Florida. There are many pages in several telephone books from Ft. Lauderdale to Homestead bearing that last name. How many telephone numbers would have to be called in such a short period of time to find the right Gonzalez person, with a nephew named Juan Miguel living in Cuba?

If the Gonzalez family did not make first contact, I would have to say it was a remarkable performance of Mr. Robert Wallis, District Director of the INS in Miami and the agents in charge of the case to locate Elian's relatives in the United States. They must have pulled together all their resources to locate the boat-wrecked boy's family in Miami.

Did Mr. Wallis or Ms. Doris Meissner, Commissioner of the INS also try to locate Juan Miguel Gonzalez, Elian's father in Cuba to learn directly from him his feelings regarding his son under INS custody, before releasing him to his great-uncle Lazaro in Miami?

Why not? The INS had in their hands a very young undocumented boy that claimed he had just lost his mother at sea after they and other Cubans left Cuba in a boat...

Wasn't the INS concerned about the immediate international complications that could develop when placing five year-old Elian under the custody of his great-uncle here in the United States, without the consent of the remaining parent, his father, living in Cuba?

On November 26th the INS released Elian to the custody of his great-uncle Lazaro Gonzalez. The very next day, the 27th, Juan Miguel Gonzalez, in Cardenas, Cuba, learned one way or another that his son was in Miami, Florida. He quickly demanded the boy be returned to him immediately. Juan Miguel complained that his ex-wife Elizabeth Brotons had taken the boy away from Cuba without his knowledge and authorization.

Why did the INS ignore the father's request? What excuse did the Miami District Director give to Juan Miguel Gonzalez for not returning Elian to him immediately?

Did anyone in the INS worry about how Fidel Castro would react when told that the authorities in the U.S. had released a young Cuban boy to some distant relatives living in Miami without the approval of his communist father?

Did the INS have any doubt that Castro would get completely involved in Elian's case, accusing the 'American imperialists' and the 'Cuban gangsters' in Miami of foul play?

Did District Director Wallis and Commissioner Meissner make the final decision all by themselves? Or did they check with and consult the Attorney General of the United States about the possibility of the serious consequences that could develop from the immediate decision they were to make?

Ms. Janet Reno was the Attorney General of the United States in charge of the Justice Department and the INS was under her jurisdiction. It was her responsibility to apply and enforce the laws of our land and the Cuban Adjustment Act determinations and dispositions as well.

Of course I am only speculating about what could have been their conversation regarding this incident. Maybe they discussed the loophole in the U.S.-Cuba migration policy allowing an intercepted refugee in need of immediate medical attention to be transported directly to any hospital in the United States.

Upon touching American soil the surviving refugee is already on U.S. territory and is allowed to request political asylum. That loophole is known by many of the Cubans adventuring into the waters of the Gulfstream, but, the request for political asylum can only be applied for when the surviving traveler is old enough to request asylum by him or herself.

Can we believe that five-year old Elian asked for political asylum? It is very unlikely he did so because, even now, he probably still doesn't know what political asylum really means. Anyway, his great-uncle Lazaro took that step on December 10, 1999 when he applied for political asylum in the United States on Elians's behalf.

As reported, political asylum was applied for exactly fifteen days after the INS had released Elian to Lazaro Gonzalez's custody, and fourteen days after Juan Miguel had demanded his son be returned to him in Cuba.

To keep the time line accurate, the following are important dates to keep in mind:

> November 26, 1999—Elian released to Lazaro Gonzalez and family.
>
> November 27, 1999—Juan Miguel Gonzalez demands the

return of his son.

December 10, 1999—Application for political asylum is filed.

What legal consultation or advice did the INS seek before accepting Elian's application for political asylum filed on his behalf by Lazaro Gonzalez knowing that the child's father had demanded that his son be returned to him in Cuba?

Did that decision come directly from the local INS office overseeing this case, or was it taken after consulting with, asking directions from and getting the approval of Attorney General Reno and the Justice Department?

Unless the District Director in Miami and his agents are used as 'scapegoats' the responsibility of this horrendous blunder rest solely in the hands of higher authorities. No agent, soldier or sailor will take any action or make a move without the orders or instructions of a supervisor, non-com or officer in the field or aboard ship.

President Harry S. Truman had a plaque adorning his desk that said it all: THE BUCK STOPS HERE.

In the Elian case, I have no doubt at all of the good intentions of those agents regarding the welfare of the boy, but we now know how traumatic and expensive that first decision taken on November 26 was. That leads all of us to a series of questions regarding the decision about the release of Elian Gonzalez and his status in the United States.

In reviewing the decision-making responsibility and the chain of command I have a few questions I would like to ask.

Did District Director Robert Wallis ask for advice from Commissioner Meissner upon learning that Elian was ready to be released from the hospital?

Did Commissioner Doris Meissner make a decision on the spot or did she consult with Attorney General Janet Reno?

Did Ms. Reno direct the BUCK to her boss, President Clinton and ask him what she should do taking under consideration the possible international complications that could develop in this case?

Did Ms. Reno follow the President's decision and execute his determination?

It is publicly known that President Clinton and Attorney General Reno have legal expertise in their background; both are lawyers. At first glance they should have realized that the illegal arrival of Elian Gonzalez to Florida (Cuban Adjustment Act, revised in 1994) and his residency in Little Havana could develop into an ugly state of affairs between the United States and Cuba, countries already at odds with each other for almost forty years.

Did the President slide the BUCK away from himself and tell his Justice Department overseer to make her own decision and determination in this case?

Would anyone admit the responsibility of this awful fiasco? I personally will not hold my breath waiting for an answer to this question.

By the way, it must be remembered that the decision to release Elian from INS custody was taken in earnest during the middle of the traditionally long weekend holiday of Thanksgiving in 1999!

4

ELIAN, HIS MIAMI FAMILY AND THE NEWS MEDIA

Lazaro Gonzalez, his wife, daughter and friends had no idea how drastically their lives would change after November 26, 1999. It is easy to picture how happy and surprised they were when the INS informed them about Elian's survival and rescue from the ocean off the east coast of Florida. The family was most likely shocked at the news and also anxious over learning that the little boy, the small son of Lazaro's nephew, was in a hospital in Hollywood. It is not hard to understand the reaction of this exiled family living in the Little Havana area in South Florida.

Did the INS notify them that Elian was going to be paroled under their custody and care while they determined the boy's status in the United States? Did Lazaro Gonzalez realize that he had no control whatsoever of future decisions of the INS? Was Lazaro told that the INS could rescind that disposition and remove Elian from their custody at any time if they reached a different decision?

I can easily guess that the single thought of taking care of a relative's child arriving to Florida under such dramatic circumstances was enough reason for the Miami family to eagerly accept the awesome responsibility placed upon them by the American authorities. The family immediately accepted the boy and made him feel wanted, and showered him with all the love, comfort and security they could offer in their home in the middle of the Cuban community in Little Havana.

Did the media immediately sense the possibility of 'big news' in the Elian case? You bet! I would wage my last two-cents they did.

The Gonzalez family's background and lifestyle was delved into, analyzed and exposed for the public to see on an almost daily basis. The reading, hearing or television watching public learned instantly who Lazaro was, from what area of Cuba he came from, when and how he arrived to the United States. We learned how old Lazaro was and what he did to support his family. Much of this information was disclosed immediately. Everyone wanted to know how Lazaro spent his spare time. How Elian was behaving and what plans Lazaro had for the future of the boy was reported as often as possible. Definitely it was news!

In a very short span of time all Cubans and other Hispanics living in South Florida and across the United States received an almost daily report of Elian and his Miami relatives. But, was anyone informed that this quite possibly could only be a temporary status for Elian to be under his great-uncle's care?

The public didn't have to wait very long before Elian himself joined Lazaro on the front page of the daily papers or on national television. Elian's legal status in the United States became a thorn in the side of many people in the United States.

Surprisingly, Lazaro's wife was spared from such scrutiny but their daughter Marisleysis, a young and beautiful lady in her early twenties, became the target of eager reporters wanting to know more about her, her father and mother. Many times and again she had to repeat how her little second cousin Elian was adapting to his new life in Miami.

Many in the news media wanted to know and report to the public. Was he missing his mother? Was Elian having any nightmares? How was Elian adapting? Was he in good health? Before the honeymoon turned into a nightmare, Marisleysis became the spokesperson for the Gonzalez family. Very soon she was categorized as Elian's surrogate mother as she was protecting him and looking out for the child's welfare at all times.

Thousands of Cuban exiles had arrived to Florida traveling in trawlers, fishing boats, or rafts before Elian did and many more after him. However, the news media has not given the same kind of coverage for others' arrivals as they did for Elian.

Was it the young age of this child that attracted the attention of so many? Or, was it the gruesome reporting of the drowning and loss of Elian's mother Elizabeth that interested the media and its audience?

Elian's picture was featured in the front page of most Miami newspapers when he was enrolled in a private school in Miami. That photo showed him wearing his new uniform. Good enough for front-page material? Some reporter followed Elian and the Gonzalez family all the way to Orlando, Florida, 200 miles from Miami. The photo of Elian's smiling face while embracing Mickey Mouse at Disney World was news, therefore, newspaper front-page material. Elian was playing with some of his new friends in the yard of his great-uncle Lazaro. That scene didn't escape the attention of an alert newspaper photographer. Front-page material?

Now, I have to ask some questions…Why did the reporters become so intensely interested in this particular case? Was it perhaps the sensationalism of reporting this case that made it so interesting? Who was behind of all this interest in Elian? Again, from whom did the news media obtain all the information as described in previous chapters? Was there a 'deep throat' living in South Florida?

Could this concentrated interest on the part of the media have been because the media wanted to feed the curiosity and appetite of the Cuban community in exile? Hardly the case! The Cubans living in the United States had quickly accepted Elian as one of their own just as they had done in many cases before him. In their minds he was one more exile rescued from the grasp of the Cuban communist authorities. As far as they knew the INS had already placed the young boy in the custody of Lazaro Gonzalez and his family, and his status in the United States depended only on filing an application for political asylum. They probably felt that the desires of Elian's mother were fulfilled. At the expense of her own life, her son was finally where she wanted him to be, in the United States of America.

My wife once told me that she noticed I have become very skeptical. I know that I am growing older and I realize that as I absorb more calendar years I am more cynical in my observations of the life around me.

Perhaps that is the reason for the following questions: Did the local and national media have any other major subject, project or case to report on? Could it be that the news medias were in such a state of withdrawal after all of the frenzy reporting of the juicy scandals coming out of the White House the previous year that they needed a story like this to get back in the running? Or could it be possible that some news' editor or publisher had an inside informer and learned that this was an emergent case that would soon reach monumental proportions?

No reporting wire was left in the cold and most of the news wire outfits were already on their toes covering the Elian case.

Charles Gibson and Diane Sawyer are co-anchors of the ABC network news early morning show, *Good Morning America*. During the tensest moments of the Elian case, *Good Morning America* sponsored on March 27 and 28, 2000 long segments in the show, interviewing Elian and his Miami family at their home in Little Havana. Present during the interviews were a psychiatrist, Dr. Gunther Perdigao and the family attorney Kendall Coffey.

In her most kindly and soft-spoken style, Diane Sawyer asked questions that were translated to the boy. I could not understand his mumbling answers in Spanish but fortunately his responses were quickly translated into English for the American audience to understand. It was very touching to see such a highly respected news personality dressed in casual attire and sitting on the floor doing the interview and playing with Elian. It was certainly well received by the Cuban community as they watched her interest and empathy for the boy and his Miami family in this unfolding drama.

Before I proceed with my narrative I have another question that I want to shake off my shoulders because it weighs on me like a ton of steel!

Did the INS investigate the "Miami" Gonzalez family before releasing Elian to their custody?

Evidently on November 26, 1999 the Gonzalez family's character, morality, finances and general standard of living were good enough for this family to be Elian's custodians. The INS did not have any reason at that time (nor anytime in the future) to believe that placing Elian under the custody of Lazaro Gonzalez would jeopardize the life of this young boy. Nothing was found that could or would disqualify him, his wife or daughter from being the proper family to look after Elian's affairs in the United States. The Gonzalez's seemed to be a very nice, neat and tightly knit family of Cuban exiles.

But, too soon though everything changed, unfortunately for the worse.

5

INS INTERVIEWS JUAN MIGUEL IN CUBA

Lazaro Gonzalez and his family were celebrating their 1999 Christmas with Elian as the center of their attention. It would be very difficult for any of them to forget any part of it, because along with the Cuban community they were waiting for the processing of the application for political asylum filed on Elian's behalf.

They must have felt sick at heart to start monitoring the actions of the Immigration and Naturalization Service when it was reported that on December 31, 1999, INS agents went to interview Juan Miguel Gonzalez in Havana, Cuba.

I don't recall any news regarding an earlier trip to Cuba by agents of the INS but through my research I found out that they had a previous interview with Juan Miguel Gonzalez at his home in Cuba, on December 13, 1999.

I am copying an excerpt from the Appeal document No 00-11424, published on June 1, 2000 by the United States Court of Appeals for the Eleventh Circuit:

> "Appeal from the United States District Court for the Southern District of Florida

> "(June 1, 2000)

> "Before EDMONDSON, DUBINA AND WILSON, Circuit Judges"

"…"An INS official, on 13 December, met with Juan Miguel at his home in Cuba. At that meeting, Juan Miguel made this comment: [Plaintiff], at the age of six, cannot make a decision on his own…I'm very grateful that he received immediate medical assistance, but he should be returned to me and my family…As for him to get asylum, I am not allowing him to stay or claim any type of petition; he should be returned immediately to me.

"Juan Miguel assured the INS official that his desire for Plaintiff's return to Cuba was genuine and was not coerced by the Cuban government…"

That trip was confirmed in a January 5th statement from the INS when they informed the parties involved of their decision that Elian "belongs with his father."

I am recalling a fact and later will ask a question: On November 27th Juan Miguel Gonzalez had requested that his son be returned to him in Cuba, but his petition fell on deaf ears. On December 13, 1999 the INS interviewed Juan Miguel at his home in Cuba at which time he reiterated that he wanted his son back.

I will copy the entire third and forth paragraphs and portions of the fifth paragraph of the Statement released on January 5, 2000 by the U.S. Department of Justice:

"During INS' two meetings with Mr. Gonzalez, his wishes for Elian were discussed at some length. He made it very clear during both of these meetings that he wants Elian returned to him as soon as possible. Based on these meetings, INS believes that he is expressing his true wishes, and therefore we have determined that Elian should be reunited with his father, Mr. Gonzalez.

"INS has advised both Mr. Gonzalez and Elian's great-uncle in Miami of this decision, and is prepared to work with all the parties involved to make the appropriate arrangements for Elian's return to his father by January 14, 2000.

"Having reached a decision, INS believes there are several ways this decision can be implemented. The United States has discussed with the Government of Cuba their consideration of allowing Mr. Gonzalez, Elian's father, to travel to the United States to accompany Elian home…"

Juan Miguel Gonzalez had stated on November 27, 1999 that he wanted his son back in Cuba. He reiterated the same request when interviewed on December 13th and one more time on December 31, 1999. On January 5, 2000 the INS informed Juan Miguel and Lazaro of their decision to return Elian to his father. Why did it take the INS from November 27, 1999 through January 5, 2000 to determine that "Elian belongs with his father"? What logical reason could they offer?

Let's assume that on November 27, 1999 the INS didn't have any proof that Juan Miguel Gonzalez was the father of Elian Gonzalez and that was why they didn't rescind the parole status of the child in the United States taking Elian back under their custody and return him to Cuba. It makes sense to think that this was the reason why an INS agent was sent to Cuba on December 13, to verify who Juan Miguel was and what rights he had to claim that Elian be returned to him. Until that time the American authorities didn't have any documentation to prove who Elian really was, to whom he belonged or who had the right to legally represent him in the U.S.

I copy again from the INS Statement dated January 5, 2000, end of the first paragraph and the entire second:

> "…"INS has determined that Mr. Juan Gonzalez of Cuba has the sole legal authority to speak on behalf of his son, Elian, regarding Elian's immigration status in the United States.
>
> "There is no question that Mr. Gonzalez is Elian's father. Moreover, Mr. Gonzalez has had a close and continuous parental relationship with his son. During INS' interviews with Elian's father, he provided vivid details about his parental relationship with his son and about the nature of the bond they share as father and son. He provided extensive documentation about Elian's schooling and his medical and health histories, as well as photographs depicting the activities in which he and his other family members frequently

participated with Elian. This scope of information and level of detail Mr. Gonzalez provided helped inform INS as to the nature and closeness of the relationship Mr. Gonzalez shared with his son Elian. INS has not uncovered any information that might call into question Mr. Gonzalez' parental and legal right with regard to Elian's immigration status."

This means that as early as December 13th and again on December 31, 1999 the INS was convinced that Juan Miguel should have absolute control of his son's future. On January 5, 2000 the INS published their decision that the only one who could request asylum on Elian's behalf was his father living in Cuba!

What was the reason for delaying the reunion of father and son until January 14? Was it because the INS wanted to give Marisleysis enough time to explain to Elian that he would be returned to Cardenas, Cuba? Was it because our government officials wanted to give the news media some extra days to fully inform the reading, listening and watching public?

Why was there so much indecision and hesitation within the INS and the Department of Justice to order Lazaro Gonzalez to return the child into the custody of the INS on January 5 instead of the 14? The INS could have and should have rescinded Elian's parole status in the U.S. and returned him to his father without any problem. Lazaro Gonzalez's lawyers didn't challenge the INS ruling in Miami-Dade circuit court until January 10, 2000, blocking Elian's return to Cuba.

For almost five months that indecisiveness haunted the federal administration and on many occasions the Attorney General tried to justify that period of time without much success in the eyes of many people.

Attorney General Reno considered Miami her hometown but she grossly overestimated her ability to influence the Cuban community in accepting the INS decision without challenging it. She should have guessed how Lazaro and the Cuban exiles would react when the INS decided that Elian belonged with his father. Did the INS or the

Department of Justice have any doubt that Lazaro Gonzalez would be advised he could and should pursue all the legal avenues at his disposal in trying to keep Elian in Miami?

All the vacillation and dilly-dallying from the Attorney General on down the line caused so many people to have teary eyes and feel anguish, while at the same time others felt anger and frustration in observing the lack of determination and inaction of the Department of Justice, one way or another.

On April 7, 2000 The Department of Justice published a Statement for immediate release from Attorney General Reno. Following are highlights of that Statement:

> "…"After meeting with Mr. Gonzalez in Cuba, INS officials also met with relatives in Miami. We wanted to give the relatives an opportunity to provide any information they could that could be relevant to the decision.
> "In January, after the interviews, the INS Commissioner announced her decision that, not only did the father speak for the son, but that the father's wishes are indeed to have his son with him.
> "From that moment, nothing prevented the United States government from immediately taking action to reunite the father and son. There was no court order. No stay. No injunction. But instead of moving hastily, we gave the relatives in Miami a chance to challenge our decision in federal court. A federal court sustained our judgment, stating 'each passing day is another day lost between Juan Gonzalez and his son.'
> "Thereafter, we again remained willing to postpone the reunion because we wanted to give the relatives every chance to argue their case in the federal appellate court. All we asked for in return was a pledge that at the end of the day—when the appeals process had run its course, the Miami relatives would turn over Elian to his father voluntarily"…"

I will recall the previous statement in another chapter when we analyze the events of April 22, 2000.

On April 13, 2000 I wrote a letter to my Representative Charles Canady. I will reprint one paragraph:

> "Time heals almost any wound if treated timely and in the proper manner. I am sure that had this situation been taken care of quickly and without hesitation, no one would be hurting as much as many are now."

When did the United States inform the Cuban government they would allow Juan Miguel to come to be reunited with his son and return immediately to his home in Cardenas, Cuba? Was it December 13th, December 31st or January 5, 2000?

What held Juan Miguel Gonzalez back from coming to Miami, Florida, get his child and return home? I have a few hypothetical scenarios regarding this question, and maybe you have one of your own...

FIRST. Initially Juan Miguel really didn't know about his ex-wife Elizabeth's plans to leave Cuba with their son Elian. He was really surprised and indignant in learning that Elian was in Miami, Florida, in the hands of his uncle Lazaro. Then, why didn't he request permission from the Cuban government to come to Miami to pick up his son on November 27, 1999 instead of asking that Elian be returned to him in Cuba?

Was it because Juan Miguel was shocked with the news about his son or was he having 'trouble' with the Cuban communist authorities before the INS agent requested to interview him at home on December 13, 1999?

Did the Cubans believe Juan Miguel when he asserted that he was absolutely unaware of his ex-wife's plans and was he having trouble convincing his 'comrades' that he had nothing to do with his son showing up in Miami?

Was the government convinced that Juan Miguel did not have any contact or relationship with any of his uncles living in Miami, FL? Later on, the news media reported that while in the United States Juan Miguel refused to have any conversation or personal contacts with his uncle Lazaro or any other Miami relative, regardless of the fact that they were taking such good care of his son Elian!

Were the interrogators trying to find out how his ex-wife Elizabeth managed to escape detection from the CDR in Cardenas, Cuba and slip away along with her son and twelve other Cubans?

Maybe Juan Miguel didn't want to rock the boat asking permission to come to Miami?

SECOND. Juan Miguel had another opportunity on December 13, 1999 or shortly after his first interview with the American authorities to ask permission to come to Miami. And a third chance, on January 14, 2000, when the INS was supposed to have Elian back under their custody.

Reader, if you were in a similar circumstance wouldn't you go to whatever length it took to go where ever your child was being held against your wishes? Yes…? Wouldn't you be at your child's side in a heartbeat?

If you said yes I agree with you, but please, let's not go too fast in this case!

There is one huge problem with this option. You would be able to do that when living in a country like ours, where you have unlimited freedom of movement and action, but that is not the case in Cuba. As a citizen of that country you can't just pack your bags and leave at any time you want to! You must heed to the rules and regulations dictated by the communist Cuban government and follow a very long and complicated procedure to secure permission to leave Cuba.

Could it be also that Juan Miguel was concerned that the CUBAN MAFIA (As Castro calls the Cubans in Miami) was going to humiliate or hurt him, maybe even kidnap him? Nonsense!

THIRD. Was Castro and his government worried about the risk of giving Juan Miguel an opportunity to defect and stay with his son in the United States if he came to Miami alone to supposedly pick up his son? Some of the Florida congressional members offered permanent residency to father and son if Juan Miguel came to the United States.

Months later, when Castro finally allowed Juan Miguel Gonzalez to come to Washington, D.C. on April 6, 2000, President Clinton was asked about his position in this case. His comment was vague as he was quoted saying, "If Juan Miguel Gonzalez wants to stay here with Elian it's okay with me."

Let's get back to the last question. Did the Cuban government not trust Juan Miguel to come for his child? It could have been a very tempting option for Juan Miguel at that time, but it is hardly the right option. He had a new wife and a new infant son and it's very unlikely he would leave them behind. Besides, his own parents, Elian's grand-parents, were also in Cardenas and he seemed satisfied with the regime controlling Cuba.

There could be a FOURTH scenario…

Even though it was reported that Juan Miguel was not coerced nor influenced by the communist government in his statements, it appears that Castro and his advisors had learned immediately of the INS com-mitment to return Elian to his father in Cuba. Could it be that Castro and his government quickly saw the possibility to embarrass the Amer-ican government, creating an international child custody case, if Elian's return to Juan Miguel was delayed for any reason?

The Cuban government could denounce the Americans for harbor-ing a bunch of 'Cuban delinquents' that had kidnapped ELIANCITO (Colloquial way used by Castro when referring to Elian) or accuse the 'Imperialists' of purposely delaying the return of the boy to his father under false pretenses that they were following the rule of law!

You can count on the fact that Castro wouldn't pass up an opportu-nity to accuse the United States of wrong doing and at the same time he (Castro) could further insult and hurt the feelings of the Cubans in exile.

It was reported, that right after learning Elian was in Miami against the wishes of his father, the communist government in Cuba organized and prompted highly politicized demonstrations all across their entire island, continuously accusing the 'American Imperialists' of holding

Elian illegally and demanding the return of the boy to his father in Cuba.

We must keep this last option in sight as we try to find an explanation to some events that started to develop in the early months of the new millennium.

In the meantime, what was the Justice Department doing?

Was Attorney General Reno seeking advice as to what to do next to appear accommodating to all parties involved? Was the Attorney General trying to conceal the mistake made in releasing Elian from the INS custody without completely analyzing all the facts in this case?

Didn't Ms. Reno learn the lesson that hesitation and lack of resolve only leads to bigger problems, sometimes with catastrophic and deadly consequences if not handled timely and properly?

It is up to you to reach your own conclusions because I cannot find a logical answer or a legitimate explanation to any of these questions.

Meanwhile, Castro must have seen the winds blowing favorably into his sails. His strategy apparently seemed to outsmart the American Administration as tension began to build-up in South Florida.

6

EXILES REACTION TO INS DETERMINATION

The Christmas holiday celebration, in most Hispanic countries, begin on December 24 and is known as 'Nochebuena' (Christmas Eve) and extend past the New Year celebrations, to January 6 with the arrival of the Three Wise Men. January 6 is the day when Cuban children find their gifts under the tree. Quite possibly Elian never received as many toys and presents as he found under his tree in Miami.

However, Lazaro Gonzalez and the Cuban exile community received an early and unwanted gift on January 5, 2000! The notification by the INS of their decision that Elian was to be returned to his father caused highly emotional reactions.

It was not very long before the Cuban community in Miami, and other Cubans across Florida, started showing up and congregating in front of Lazaro's home in Little Havana to express their support for the Gonzalez family. Cubans of all ages, from all social, political and economic status were making appearances and carrying posters pleading the INS to reverse the decision to return Elian to Cuba. Many made eloquent and emotional homilies pleasing the crowd present. The American and Cuban flags were always seen waving in the background while the news media continuously reported the poignant but non-violent demonstrations.

During the peak of the tension caused by the Elian case, 12th Street between 23rd and 24th Avenues in northwest Miami where the Gonzalez family lived was closed to vehicular traffic. Barricades were erected to keep the excited Cuban community crowd from blocking the entrance to the family's home. The situation at hand reaching its climax in April of 2000 saw many public figures making passionate and moving speeches, offering their support for Lazaro Gonzalez's efforts to keep Elian in the U.S.

Local radio stations dedicated many hours on a daily basis to interview supporters and air opinions from who ever wanted to offer one. It was rare a day that the newspapers didn't inform the Miamians of what was happening in this case.

Just a few days before the federal authority's forceful action of April 22, 2000, Miami-Dade County Mayor, Alex Penelas declared in a news conference and to the crowd gathered on 'Lazaro's street' that his Metro Police Department would not assist any federal agent in taking Elian away from Miami by force. He also warned that he would hold President Clinton and Attorney General Janet Reno responsible for any violence in Miami. Was he boasting in front of the crowds and cameras to improve his ratings? None of the members of the Metro-Dade law enforcement agency were seen in the area in the early hours of April 22, 2000.

Miami City Mayor, Joe Carollo, was also interviewed by television networks and publicly declared that the Miami police force was there just to protect the demonstrators and to keep everything orderly. After the raid was over Mayor Carollo chastised his own Police Chief for helping the federal agents in the raid.

Singer of international fame, Gloria Estefan, was there to the cheering of the Cuban exile community and others, showing her full support to the cause.

Many well-known figures were there, such as Congresswoman Ileana Ros-Lehtinen and Congressman Lincoln Diaz-Balart. It is not my intention to try and recount all of them but I am sure their contributions to the effort to keep Elian in the United States will never be forgotten by the Gonzalez family and the Cuban community in exile.

I must add that none of the officers of Metro-Dade or Miami police departments had any major confrontations or made arrests of the spontaneous group of demonstrators.

I am sure the reader will understand and appreciate that I am not violating my promise of not forcing my opinion about any particular situation, but I believe this is an appropriate spot to include some excerpts from an extensive letter I sent to my congressman in Washington, D.C. In the letter I tried to explain some of the reasons for the position the Cubans in Miami have regarding the Elian case. There are not that many Cubans in his 12th District in Central Florida!

On April 13, 2000 I wrote:

> "...It must be noted that the emotional and vocal Cuban community that oppose Elian's return knows firsthand the hardships involved in living under a totalitarian regime as the one imposed in communist Cuba. Castro has found a way to further irritate the Cubans here by showing his supposed concern for family. Many of them still have relatives in Cuba that have not been able to leave the red paradise because of the communist ruling and oppressive polices.
>
> "...He (Castro) will use every angle he can to appear to be the family-oriented leader he is not.
>
> "Some of his own relatives (Castro's) asked for political asylum and ran away from him.
>
> "...I must conclude this lengthy letter by trying to explain the loudly vocal and emotional Cuban feelings regarding this case (Elian's) and of any other one involving Castro and his regime.
>
> "Think of an unlikely and impossible change of our form of government in the United States. Suppose that a dictator forcibly replaces our democratic system and his ruling is imposed over everyone here. Shortly after taking over, the new government confiscates all personal land, property and businesses without proper compensation.
>
> "Worse! They tell you where to live, where you can work and how to educate your children. Some of those that refuse to accept the new rules are executed or imprisoned. Others are forced to leave

the land of their birth and live in a foreign land.

"How do you think the politically exiled American would feel when anything happened in their new country involving anything regarding the dictator that pushed them out from their native land?

"The answer to this hypothetical situation will explain the Cuban exile's feeling about Castro, his cohorts and the communist regime they represent and force on their suffered captive island."

Throughout the previous excerpt I tried to describe the loud and emotional Cuban exiles that were featured on TV news and/or front pages of newspapers. Although Castro characterizes them as the CUBAN MAFIA, CUBAN GANGTERS or CUBAN GUSANOS, I hope you had an opportunity to see photos in your local newspapers or saw on television when they were reporting on the rallies and demonstrations in front of Lazaro's home. The weapons they carried to their protest vigils were only that of their emotions, religious medals, posters, and rosaries. There were no insulting slogans, no obscene screams or gestures, no arrests, no violence and no public destruction or disorder at all!

The majority of Cubans in exile are very emotional, but definitely law-abiding persons with a high respect for authority, especially those in uniform. Unfortunately, there are some exceptions to this statement, but truly a very small number. They are very politically opinionated, extremely passionate in their beliefs and while expressing their ideas they can give you a good piece of their mind. But also, when the time comes they will listen to and respect the opinions of others with different points of view.

Do they have a loud mouth? Yes…Absolutely! Are they verbally offensive or abusive? Very unlikely, but when teased enough they will respond accordingly, as the situation might demand.

Are the Cubans aggressive by nature? No more or no less than any other red-blooded person.

I believe I can honestly describe a typical Cuban, regardless of gender, because before I became an American citizen I was one of them. I was born in Havana, Cuba.

7

ARENA READY FOR LEGAL WRANGLING

Do you remember the question I raised in Chapter Five, FOURTH scenario, regarding one of the possible reasons why Juan Miguel Gonzalez did not come to Miami immediately to rescue his son from the hands of his uncle Lazaro?

I believe that the FOURTH scenario began to unfold when the American authorities set the stage for Castro to develop his plan: to blame the U.S. of playing dirty. He increased his well known grumbling tactics as he began complaining about how Elian's case was progressing. But at no time did Castro mention his knowledge of the commitment the INS and the Department of Justice made to reunite father and son. For his political advantage, Castro never uttered a single word about it during his denunciation of foul play by the Americans and the CUBAN MAFIA.

I will repeat the question again because it seems to properly fit into the developing saga of Elian's custody case: Could it be that when Castro and his advisors 'learned' right after the meetings in Cuba of the INS commitment to return Elian to his father in Cuba, they saw a big opportunity to embarrass the American government by creating an international child custody case?

The Cuban government would have a field day if Elian's return to Juan Miguel were delayed for a while.

The hesitation of the Justice Department to enforce the decision made by the INS on January 5, 2000 to return Elian to his father on the 14th of the same month played right into Castro's hands and set off the FOURTH scenario. That hesitation also had given Lazaro time to file a lawsuit on January 10, 2000 against the INS decision, and a few days later on the 19th in a federal court, tying up the Attorney General's office resources with defending their action in court proceedings.

On January 19th, as Lazaro's attorneys filed his lawsuit against the INS in federal court, the Department of Justice issued the following statement:

> "DEPARTMENT OF JUSTICE AND IMMIGRATION AND NATURALIZATION SERVICE JOINT STATEMENT ON FEDERAL COURT REGARDING ELIAN GONZALEZ.
> "Attorneys in Miami have filed a federal district court action related to the INS decision regarding Elian Gonzalez. The U.S. department of Justice (DOJ) and the Immigration and Naturalization Service (INS) are fully prepared to quickly respond to this action.
> "It is important for the well-being of Elian Gonzalez that the status of this 6-year-old boy be resolved as quickly as possible. We will therefore ask the court to expeditiously address this matter. Last week INS decided to extend the January date for the reunification of Elian Gonzalez with his father in order to accommodate federal court action.
> "On January 4, INS determined that Juan Gonzalez, the father of Elian Gonzalez, has the sole legal authority to speak for his son on immigration issues. This decision was based on the facts and the law, and recognizes the bond that exists between parent and child. Last week Attorney General Janet Reno reaffirmed her support for the INS decision.
> "In keeping with normal DOJ and INS policy, we will not publicly discuss the specifics of issues pending before the courts."

Although the Department of Justice requested that "the court expeditiously address this matter," did Attorney General Reno, an experienced prosecutor ever consider the possibility that even having the law of the land on her side, the Elian case could drag on for quite a while in the courts through appeals? Did she ever think this case might possibly go all the way to the Supreme Court of the United States? She must have been aware of the caliber and expertise of the team of lawyers representing Lazaro Gonzalez.

Castro and the Cuban communist government were already at full speed, loudly complaining against the United States and he continued his quest to outsmart the Justice Department and the Clinton Administration. Castro grabbed the opportunity to accuse the CUBAN GANGSTERS in Miami of kidnapping Elian.

To further his claim, Castro was ready to send his scouts to test the American public's opinion in the Elian affair by involving the boy's grandmothers. I dedicate the next chapter to describe the effectiveness and reactions to the grandmothers' appearance on stage.

On February 18, 2000 the Department of Justice released a statement responding to several requests from Juan Miguel while he was still in Cuba.

"INS RESPONSE TO MR. JUAN GONZALEZ.

"The U.S. Immigration and Naturalization Service (INS) today informed Mr. Juan Gonzalez, father of Elian Gonzalez, that the INS remains fully committed to reuniting him with his son Elian as soon as possible, consistent with legal procedures. The INS told Mr. Gonzalez that after careful consideration of his request to move Elian, the agency does not plan to change the temporary care arrangements for Elian at this time.

"The decision was made in response to requests from Juan Gonzalez that Elian be moved from the care of Lazaro Gonzalez and placed in the care of Manolo Gonzalez, both of whom are Juan Gonzalez's uncles. INS emphasized to Mr. Gonzalez that Elian's current care arrangements are only temporary while a federal court reviews INS' decision. INS stated that the agency shares Mr. Gonzalez's concern that Elian be well cared for, and therefore will request information from Lazaro Gonzalez concerning the credentials of any psychiatrist or psychologist who has seen Elian, as well as an explanation of any treatment that may have been prescribed for him. INS also will request information regarding Elian's schooling.

"The INS advised Juan Gonzalez that a Miami-based nongovernmental organization conducted a post-placement visit to verify that Lazaro Gonzalez's home was an adequate setting for Elian's temporary care. INS indicated that transferring Elian temporarily to a new and unfamiliar environment would not be advisable for the child after already experiencing the trauma of leaving his home in Cuba and losing his mother. Instead, INS will continue to focus its efforts on returning Elian to his father.

"INS also stated that it is aware of Lazaro Gonzalez's past convictions for driving under the influence of alcohol, but that the information INS has at present does not suggest that Lazaro Gonzalez's home is not an adequate environment for Elian's temporary care at this time. INS is prepared, however, to revisit this issue if additional relevant information becomes available.

"Regarding Mr. Gonzalez's concern about the Miami family's request that the federal district court appoint a 'guardian ad litem' for Elian, INS stated that the Government is preparing a response to that motion which will be filed with the court within the next few days.

"INS reiterated to Mr. Gonzalez that it is committed to resolving this matter as fairly and expeditiously as possible."

The words in these statements were music to Castro's ears. The delay of Elian's return played right into Castro's plans to further humiliate the United States. As you can gather from the reading of these two statements, the DOJ played right into Castro's hands. I am sure that Castro enjoyed every single line of them.

Reader, am I too far off course?

8

GRANDMOTHERS IN TOWN

On January 21, 2000 a new development beset an episode of the Elian case. Mariela Quintana, mother of Juan Miguel, and Raquel Rodriguez, mother of Elizabeth arrived in New York City. They are Elian's grandmothers. Oden Marichal, representing the Cuban Council of Churches and a known member of the Cuban National Assembly, a communist party man, escorted them.

What were the grandmothers reason for coming to the United States? According to the determination of the INS on January 5, 2000 only Juan Miguel Gonzalez could represent his son in any legal matter in the United States.

Juan Miguel and Castro had assurances from the INS and the Department of Justice that Elian would be sent back to them as soon as the legal webs were cleared up. The most formidable team of lawyers represented Castro and Juan Miguel in the United States court system. The legal staff of the Immigration and Naturalization Service was advocates for them, with the Attorney General of the United States and the Justice Department as a back-up squad.

So, why did the grandmothers need to come so suddenly to the United States? Did they want to see their grandchild personally? To make sure that he was in good health and had been treated and fed properly? That his schooling was progressing?

Or, were they following marching orders received from Castro in his attempt to further incite the passion of the Cuban exiles, while appealing to the family and sentimental values of concerned American citizens?

Was the Cuban government promoting more embarrassment to the United States by the two grandmothers imploring for the return of their grandchild to his father in Cuba?

On January 22, 2000, the day after their arrival, Mariela Quintana, Raquel Rodriguez and Oden Marichal met with Attorney General Reno and INS Commissioner Doris Meissner in Washington, D.C. The grandmothers went to that meeting with Dr. Joan Brown Campbell, (their hostess during their visit to the United States), Bob Edgar and Oscar Bolioli, of the National Council of Churches.

As a result of that meeting, a news release from the Department of Justice was issued:

> "FOR IMMEDIATE RELEASE
> "January 22, 2000
> "Attorney General and Commissioner Meissner Statement
> "Washington, D.C.—Attorney General Janet Reno and I.N.S. Commissioner Doris Meissner met today with Mariela Quintana, Raquel Rodriguez, grandmothers of Elian Gonzalez, and Dr. Joan Brown Campbell, Bob Edgar and Oscar Bolioli, of the National Council of Churches, as well as Oden Marichal of the Cuban Council of Churches.
> "The Attorney General and Commissioner Meissner issued the following statement:
> "Ms. Quintana and Ms. Rodriguez made a very compassionate and heartfelt plea to be reunited with their grandson. They asked when Elian could return to his father and the rest of his family in Cuba. We explained that this matter is now in federal court but that we will seek resolution as expeditiously as possible. We accepted a letter from Ms. Quintana and Ms. Rodriguez which reiterated the issues raised in today's meeting. We maintain that the law recognizes the unique relationship between parent and child and that family reunification has long been a cornerstone of both American immigration law and INS practice."

Why did the National Council of Churches become involved in this case? The National Council of Churches and the Cuban Council of Churches had joined forces with Juan Miguel and the Cuban communist government, strongly campaigning for a quick return of Elian to Cardenas, Cuba.

On January 5, 2000, The Guardian published an article written by Tom Gibb in Havana, I quote:

> "..."Leaders of the US Council of Churches, which represents 35 protestant churches, traveled on Monday to Elian's home town of Cardenas to meet his father. Juan Miguel Gonzalez has demanded his son's return ever since Elian was rescued by Florida fishermen after spending two days clinging to an inner tube.
>
> "He is currently with a great uncle in Florida who, backed by Cuban-American politicians, wants him to be given political asylum in the U.S. But the powerful US Council of Churches thinks this would not be in the boy's best interest.
>
> "We are more convinced than ever that this boy belongs with his family in Cuba,' said Dr. Joan Brown Campbell, who heads the church delegation. Speaking from Elian's father's home, she said Elian had a loving family in Cuba, who were more than capable of looking after him, and she appealed for President Bill Clinton to intervene.
>
> "We have to help our president see that the issue is a moral one—not political," she said. But at this stage, that has become very difficult, a crowd in Cardenas carrying placards with Elian's photograph saying "Free Elian" met the church leaders.
>
> "Havana has accused Miami exiles of kidnapping and psychologically torturing the boy, rallies demanding his return are continuing, and the government has printed hundreds of thousands of T-shirts and posters. The issue has also dominated television and radio."..."

Chris Weinkopf, managing editor of FrontPageMag, wrote an article on January 11, 2000 titled *Elian Gonzalez and Fidel's Useful Idiots.* I quote:

"…"The National Council of Churches, flagship of the underreported Religious Left. The Council has played an active role in the Gonzalez controversy, sending its outgoing general secretary down to Cuba to announce, much to Castro's delight, that it supports Elian's return. The Council is a reliable champion of the Castro regime. Just last year, its secretary general asked an audience in Havana, with Fidel Castro beaming in the front row, to forgive the American people for the U.S. embargo against their country."…"

The 64th General Synod of the Bible Presbyterian Church held a meeting August 3-8, 2000 and adopted Resolution 64:11.

I copy excerpts of that Resolution:

"On the N.C.C. or "The National Council of Castroites"
"In a recent article by Cal Thomas, published in the May/June 2000 "Presbyterian Layman" he wrote that when Joan Brown Campbell became head of the National Council of Churches in 1993, she said, "We did not understand the depth of the suffering of Christians under communism. And we failed to really cry out against communist oppression." However, she and the N.C.C. have continued to demonstrate their support of communism in the recent Elian Gonzalez affair. Thomas further wrote, "Now, given an opportunity to cry out against the communist oppression of Christians in Cuba and Castro's numerous other violations of human rights, Campbell has aligned herself with the oppressors and directed her invective toward her own country." Mark Tooley, in the publication Heterodoxy says that Campbell has "praised Cuba for having made a 'priority of caring for the poor,' while failing to point out that Castro and the communist system in Cuba are responsible for much of the poverty in that nation. We also would take note that Bible distribution is forbidden in Cuba."…"

I can't help but ask the following question because it erupts from me like melting lava from a volcano!

Is there any logical explanation as to why Dr. Joan Brown Campbell of the National Council of Churches, a religious organization representing Christian protestant churches, defended and is advocate for a government that bases its dictatorship on communism?

Castro's government follows the guidelines of Marx and Lenin and teaches their communist atheist/materialist doctrine. In that doctrine any mention of God, or as a matter of fact any god, is forbidden! On December 2, 1961 Fidel Castro himself admitted that he was a marxist-leninist, and that he had always been one and will always be one for the rest of his days!

I am sure the meeting on January 22nd at the Justice Department in Washington, D.C. was remarkable considering those in attendance. I still question why it was necessary for the representatives of the religious organizations to attend a conference between the Cuban grandmothers and the Attorney General of the United States.

Were the expenses of Dr. Joan Brown Campbell, Bob Edgar, Oscar Bolioli and especially Oden Marichal coming from Cuba, paid for by funds of the National Council of Churches or from donations and contributions by the parishioners of the churches forming that council?

The cost of traveling for Mariela and Raquel to New York, Washington, D.C., Miami and Miami Beach plus food and incidentals for the two grandmothers alone ran into some money, and that is not counting the cost of the winter wardrobe required for both of them. Surely they would not need such warm clothing in the moderate Cuban climate…

Besides those expenses the time and money spent by the U.S. Attorney General and the INS Commissioner could also add up to a tidy sum.

All this activity for the two grandmothers to deliver a letter to the Attorney General and inquire, "When Elian could return to his father and the rest of his family in Cuba?"

A telephone call and a few cents stamp could have had the same results as the trip of the two grandmothers…"Elementary, Dr. Watson, elementary."

Meanwhile, it is easy to understand that while in Washington, D.C., Mariela, Raquel and Oden immediately established contact with Cuban government representatives in that city. Jose Imperatori, a Cuban diplomat holding the rank of Second Secretary of the Cuban Interests Section in Washington, D.C. was designated to go with the two Cuban grandmothers to meet Elian in Miami, Florida.

The grandmothers certainly had secured a dubious escort from the Cuban Interests Section! It was reported that the United States government accused Imperatori of espionage…Later on the Department of State ordered him out of the country!

On January 24th, Mariela and Raquel flew to Miami to see Elian. They refused to visit him at his Little Havana home. Why? Were they afraid that the Cuban exiles demonstrating near the home would attack them? Whatever their reason they returned to Washington, D.C. without seeing their grandson.

Sister Jeanne O'Laughlin, President of the prestigious Barry College, located in Miami Shores, graciously accepted a request from her old friend Attorney General Janet Reno and agreed to host a meeting at her home in Miami Beach for Mariela and Raquel's meeting with Elian on January 26, 2000. I have no doubt that Sister O'Laughlin had arranged for the meeting to be in the most pleasant atmosphere possible.

Hopefully the two grandmothers were pleased when they finally saw that their grandson was in good physical condition, well groomed and possibly better dressed than when he lived in Cardenas, Cuba.

Besides Sister O'Laughlin, Mariela Quintana, Raquel Rodriguez and Attorney General Reno, who else was present when Elian faced his two grandmothers for the first time since November 22, 1999? Was Commissioner Meissner a witness to that encounter? Did Dr. Joan Brown Campbell, Bob Edgar or Oden Marichal attended that meeting? Was Jose Imperatori there or was he on his way back to Cuba already?

Sister O'Laughlin's statements after the meeting received harsh criticism from the National Council of Churches as well as from Ms. Maxine Waters, Representative from the State of California.

On January 28th, ABCNews.com reported:

> "..."Before the Wednesday 26th meeting Sister Jeanne O'Laughlin's opinion was, 'I would go with the law that the child should be with the father, but what I saw and felt really frightened me for the child.' The nun who hosted the reunion between Elian Gonzalez and his grandmothers, now believes Congress should make the boy a U.S. citizen. 'I'm no longer neutral,' O'Laughlin told reporters after the meeting with Reno..."
>
> "..."Also today, the nun met with Sen. Connie Mack, the Florida Republican who is the chief backer of making the 6-year-old Cuban boy an American, and said she would help with Mack's cause. 'I still believe that it is best for him to remain in this country,' she said following her meeting with Mack."...
>
> "..."The National Council of Churches said it was 'surprised' that O'Laughlin chose to step out of her assigned role of neutrality. We regret that Sister Jeanne, in choosing to state her opinion after exercising the role of neutral host so admirably, has in her action further fueled the fire of controversy and eliminated herself as a neutral facilitator in any future discussions on this matter."..."

Why did the representative from the State of California, Maxine Waters, get involved in the Elian case? Previous to the Elian controversy, Maxine Waters had received permission by the communist government to visit Cuba. What did she learn from those trips that made Congresswoman Waters an expert in Cuban affairs?

She was quoted in the ABCNews.com report as saying,

> "I am bewildered. Never in my wildest imagination would I think that a nun who was supposed to be neutral party would undermine that neutrality."

Why was the National Council of Churches 'surprised' and Congresswoman Walters 'bewildered' with Sister O'Laughlin's comments and statement?

Sister O'Laughlin had all the right to exercise her 'freedom of speech' and her right 'to petition the Government for a redress of grievances' granted to her by the First Amendment to the Constitution of the United States of America. Hurray for this courageous nun!

At this time I would like for us to borrow the hand held time-leaping machine used in the popular science-fiction television series *Quantum Leap*. Let us be transported back to the year 1864. We find ourselves living in the middle of Washington, D.C. society.

We learn through the newspapers that a slave mother and her son had escaped from a Southern plantation and they had headed north. The reporters further inform us that both of them had attempted to cross the Potomac River. Tragically the mother drowned in the swift currents, and one way or another her young son managed to stay afloat. While fishing from the north side of the river, soldiers of the Union forces of General Ulysses S. Grant spotted the boy and pulled him to safety.

I want to know which religious organization, elected politician or appointed member of the administration of President Abraham Lincoln would have the nerve to ask the President, or his Attorney General Edward Bates, to send the child back to the landlord of the plantation, who also owned the father...

Activating the time machine we jump forward to the year 2000 to return home...

What took place during that meeting that caused Sister O'Laughlin to change her opinion about Elian's status in the U.S.?

In my research I found an article written by Mindy Belz titled *"All Expenses Paid—Greg Craig's Funny Money Deal with ADM Methodist Church and Castro"* published in World Magazine on May 13, 2000. I quote:

"…"In an affidavit filed in federal district court subsequent to the meeting in her home, Ms. O'Laughlin said, 'It was clear from my observations that the Cuban government was exerting control over Elian's grandmothers and the National Council of Churches.' She said Mr. Edgar helped her reach that conclusion. Mr. Edgar told her that he felt 'Castro himself was calling the shots.' Cuban officials, he said, 'dissuaded and frightened the grandmothers from visiting the Miami relatives' home,' reads Ms. O'Laughlin's sworn statement."…"

Why didn't the INS or Attorney General Reno make a statement about the meeting with Mariela, Raquel and Elian? Did Attorney General Reno need time to analyze and think about the scene she witnessed in Miami Beach? Was the Attorney General surprised by the comments of her friend, Sister O'Laughlin? To my knowledge, the INS or Justice Department released no official statement regarding that meeting.

I learned three things from the Miami Beach meeting.

ONE. Sister Jeanne O'Laughlin said she initially favored returning the boy to his father, but after witnessing the meeting she supported the idea of keeping Elian in Miami.

TWO. Elian himself was featured in the news saying "La Vieja quiere que yo me vaya pa' Cuba, pero yo no quiero volver pa' Cuba." Translated: "The old lady wants that I go back to Cuba, but I don't want to go back to Cuba." Without being disrespectful to any of the ladies attending that meeting, to whom was Elian referring to? Some people claim that Elian was instructed to say that, but others insisted that the statement came from Elian himself, without any prompting or coaching.

THREE. Abuela Mariela and Abuela Raquel returned to Cuba to a hero's welcome by a crowd of demonstrators at the airport in Havana, Cuba.

What information did Mariela and Raquel give to Castro, Juan Miguel and the Cubans congregated at the airport after their trip to see ELIANCITO? That they delivered the letter personally to the Attorney

General of the United States and they finally saw Elian in Miami Beach, away from Lazaro Gonzalez and his family in Little Havana?

Did they say anything different from what Castro had been telling the Cuban people in order to incite their emotions?

Did the grandmothers accomplish their mission? That depends on what their mission was. Some have the opinion that the grandmothers won a delay in the congressional action to make Elian a United States citizen while they visited with congressional representatives that favored the side of the Cuban father and Castro.

Was information given to the crowd at the airport about any possible success in the public relations aspect of this trip to the 'hated' United States?

Can you see the FOURTH scenario developing…?

9

FATHER HIRES AMERICAN LAWYER

It must have felt like a slap in the face to Attorney General Janet Reno in learning that Dr. Joan Brown Campbell of the National Council of Churches had contacted The Rev. Dr. Thom White Wolf Fassett, General Secretary of The General Board of Church and Society of The United Methodist Church and that both had the intention of hiring Gregory B. Craig as the personal lawyer for Juan Miguel Gonzalez.

Did Drs. Campbell and Fassett make that decision after witnessing the grandmothers' visit with their grandson Elian in Miami Beach on January 26, 2000 and being 'surprised' by Sister O'Laughlin's forceful statements to the news media? Were these religious representatives concerned by the lack of comments from the INS and Attorney General Janet Reno?

Why? Did they really believe that the Attorney General's efforts were not sufficient to reunite Elian with his father in Cuba?

The General Board of Church and Society of The United Methodist Church released this press statement:

> "March 10, 2000
> "The General Board of Church and Society Supports Legal Representation for the Father of Elian Gonzalez.
> "The Rev. Dr. Joan Brown Campbell, former General Secretary of the National Council of Churches and The Rev. Dr. Thom White Wolf Fassett, General Secretary of The General Board of Church and Society of The United Methodist Church, approached Gre-

gory B. Craig, of the law firm of Williams and Connolly, over three weeks ago to enlist his representation for Juan Miguel Gonzalez, the father of Elian Gonzalez.

"Dr. Campbell, while General Secretary of the National Council of Churches, initiated the Council's engagement with the Elian Gonzalez case. The request for involvement was initiated by the Cuban Council of Churches. During their U.S. visit, the grandmothers stayed with Campbell in her home. Dr. Campbell has maintained a close relationship with the Gonzalez family and has continued to work for the return of Elian to his father.

"Both Campbell and Fassett were concerned about adequate representation for Juan Miguel Gonzalez here in the United States. They approached Gregory Craig who agreed to explore this role with the family and the Cuban authorities. A trip to Cuba was planned. From the beginning it was important to gain the trust of Juan Miguel and his family and to gain the assurance that any legal counsel would have direct access to Gonzalez without interference.

"Campbell, Fassett, Craig and an associate traveled to Cuba to meet with Cuban officials and Juan Miguel Gonzalez and the entire family to verify that there was unimpeded access to the father and that the family was free to decide upon the engagement of legal counsel. Mr. Craig has now been asked by Juan Miguel to play that role.

"The General Board of Church and Society is paying for the services of Gregory Craig through a humanitarian fund established by the board executive committee to receive voluntary contributions as a means of providing fair and equal treatment for the father of Elian Gonzalez under the law in the United States court.

"Contact: Dr. Thom White Wolf Fassett at 202-488-5623

"Dr. Joan Brown Campbell at 716-357-6274"

Did Drs. Campbell and Fassett seriously consider the performance of the attorneys and legal staff of the INS and the Department of Justice to be inadequate?

Evidently both Dr. Campbell and Dr. Fassett reached the conclusion that Juan Miguel needed his own lawyer to expedite the return of his son. Did the religious representatives discuss with Gregory Craig the possibility of starting legal action themselves?

We should remember what Dr. Campbell said on January 3, 2000, speaking in front of a crowd while visiting Juan Miguel in Cardenas, Cuba. She commented that the case at hand needed to be brought to the attention of President Clinton as a moral issue, not political, and she suggested she would appeal for the President to intervene.

Did Dr. Campbell have enough clout to reach the President of the United States? I don't know.

It is not my intention in any way to diminish the abilities of the candidate of Drs. Campbell and Fassett, but I wonder, why out of the numerous brilliant and famous attorneys in the United States, including Gregory Craig, did they specifically select and hand pick him?

Was Mr. Craig known for his experience in immigration cases and/or international child custody litigations?

He seems to be a talented and able jurist, but could his choosing have been because he was a personal friend of William J. Clinton? Gregory Craig had represented the President as his legal counsel during the impeachment hearings in front of the Judiciary Committee of the House of Representatives.

I am sure that President Clinton would speak with Mr. Craig any time he called the White House.

Could this be a different angle to the FOURTH scenario?

In the meantime, while all this traveling to Cuba and back to the United States by Dr. Campbell and her entourage was taking place, the attorneys of the INS with the complete support of the DOJ were involved in a full-fledged legal battle with Lazaro Gonzalez and his lawyers since January 10, 2000.

The lawsuit against the INS and Attorney General Reno was filed first in a Miami-Dade Circuit Court of the State of Florida and later in a U.S. Federal Circuit Court, on January 19, 2000. The INS did not recognize the authority of the state court to hear or rule on federal immigration matters.

U.S. District Judge William M. Hoeveler was designated to hear the case. To expedite the proceedings he moved the date of the hearing up from March 6 to February 22, 2000 to accommodate the INS request to have a quick ruling on this case. However, on February 20 Judge Hoeveler suffered a moderate stroke and was hospitalized.

U.S. District Chief Judge, Edward B. Davis, after talking to the doctors for Judge Hoeveler decided to select, by a random lottery system, another judge to preside over the Lazaro Gonzalez lawsuit.

U.S. District Judge K. Michael Moore was selected, but because his docket was already full the hearing had to be rescheduled again to the original date of March 6, 2000.

I took the painstaking task of researching the chronological order of all those dates for the legal hearings on Lazaro's federal lawsuit against the INS and Attorney General Reno because something was amiss…

The General Board of Church and Society of The United Methodist Church had offered to pay the tab for the legal fees of Gregory Craig through voluntary contributions to a humanitarian fund established by the board executive, and Juan Miguel agreed to have Gregory Craig representing him in the United States on March 10, 2000.

I find it very strange that Juan Miguel Gonzalez, still in Cuba, asked Gregory Craig, back in the United States, to "provide him fair and equal treatment under the law in the United States courts." The proceeding in the U.S. Federal District Court regarding the status of Elian in the United States was already under way, starting on March 6, 2000.

Hello…Am I missing something here?

I admit that I do not have any legal expertise, but it is clear to me that Mr. Craig could not do that much to accelerate the reunion of his new Cuban client with his son. Would the U.S. District Court of the United States allow him to jump in the middle of the hearing alleging he was the legal representative of the father of the child that was the center of the litigations?

Or, did he offer his help and legal expertise to the INS and the Department of Justice? Why not, they were on the same side, and the more the merrier.

Was Mr. Craig contemplating the idea of recommending that his client sue Lazaro Gonzalez in criminal court for holding Elian in his Miami home against the child's father's wishes? Kidnapping a child is a very serious offense in the United States!

As it was explained in the March 10th Statement from the General Board of Church and Society of The Methodist Church, one of the conditions Gregory Craig stipulated in accepting Juan Miguel as his client was to have direct and unimpeded access to him without interference from anyone. But, did or did not Juan Miguel actually need to report to Castro or his representatives in the Cuban Interests Section in Washington, D.C. of any conversation, move or action before it was taken?

By the way, how did Gregory Craig communicate with Juan Miguel and his family in Cuba? Did he or any of the other Americans that traveled to Cuba on this matter speak fluent Spanish?

Can I assume that Dr. Campbell had enough control of the Spanish language when she delivered her pro-Castro regime rhetoric in her speech to the Cuban audience there? Did she have that extra duty to perform?

On the other hand, if they did not speak Spanish, did the Cuban authorities supply a 'trustful' interpreter?

What about the time spent while in the United States? Was the possible language barrier overcome with the help of a Cuban from the Interests Section in Washington, D.C. fulfilling that task?

I admit that I am at a loss! Some of the previous questions could have a simple and logical explanation, but I can't find any satisfactory answers to many of them.

Anyway, as the events began unfolding at a fairy fast pace, it seems that Juan Miguel's American lawyer's expected performance and role was clearly leaning more toward 'procurement and public relations' duties than actual 'legal representation' in the courts of the United States.

10

BEFORE JUAN MIGUEL'S ARRIVAL

How many of those demonstrating in Cuba wearing the T-shirts supplied by the communist Cuban government and waving the posters calling to FREE ELIAN wished to be in the boy's little shoes, walking freely in Miami, Florida?

How many of the demonstrators were there because they were afraid not to be there? I can assure you the numbers would be astonishing!

It's not hard to believe that many of the people in those crowds were dreaming of wearing the same American clothes as Elian was wearing. Eating as much as Elian was eating…Many of them certainly would like to buy the most basic staples without waiting in line for hours and restricted by the rationing of "La Libreta" (Cuban rations and allowance book). And above all, they probably wanted to voice their true feelings without fear of retaliation and punishment from the communist authorities!

On March 21, 2000 ABCNews.com published an article by a reporter from Reuters from Havana:

> "Cubans reacted with delight today at a U.S. judge's ruling against the Miami relatives of shipwreck survivor Elian Gonzalez, and expressed hope the boy may return soon…"

A paragraph toward the end of the report probably expresses the feelings of many of the demonstrators participating in the 'spontaneous' rallies in Cuba:

"…'Let's hope this situation finally gets resolved, because we can't take any more of this, it's the only thing we hear at breakfast, lunch and dinner, the same thing every day,' said a 28-year-old-cook, who asked not to be named."

Not a very enthusiastic declaration coming from a Cuban national who marched through the city to end in a 'spontaneous' demonstration in front of the old United States Embassy building, now housing the American Interests Section in Havana. Sure makes me wonder how staged the demonstrations were.

No doubt there were some true believers in those crowds but I find it hard to believe that the populace chanting in Havana streets "FREE ELIAN, FREE ELIAN" had any choice in the matter.

Back from a nightmare to reality…

The lawsuit heard by U.S. District Judge K. Michael Moore did not produce the results wanted by Lazaro and his lawyers. The INS determination of January 5, 2000 was upheld and affirmed in court by a ruling on March 21, 2000 and Judge Moore was quoted in his ruling:

"Determination to grant asylum is a matter within the discretion of the attorney general."

We already knew how the Attorney General felt; Elian belonged with his father. District Court Judge Moore was further quoted:

"Each passing day is another day lost between Juan Gonzalez and his son."

Lazaro's lawyers appealed that ruling in the United States Court of Appeals for the Eleventh Circuit, in Atlanta, Georgia with hearings on May 11, 2000.

In the meantime, the INS and the Department of Justice invigorated by the U.S. court's favorable decision were in constant discussions and negotiations with Lazaro and his lawyers. The main issues brought up and discussed throughout theses meetings were the ramifications of the termination of the parole status and the release of Elian from his great-uncle's custody.

I reproduce entirely the following statement because I want to comment about its content, and compare it with the following statement from the same U.S. government department.

"U.S. DEPARTMENT OF JUSTICE
"IMMIGRATION AND NATURALIZATION SERVICE
"Washington, D.C. 20536
"STATEMENT
"March 28, 2000
"ELIAN GONZALEZ
"Officials representing the Department of Justice and the Immigration and Naturalization Service met with attorneys representing Lazaro Gonzalez this morning at the INS District Office in Miami. The purpose of the meeting was to discuss the ramifications of parole termination and the orderly return of Elian to his father including, most importantly, measures to ensure that Elian's transfer occur in a manner that is sensitive to his needs.

"While INS has always had the authority to implement its decision, we have gone to great lengths to bring about a resolution that is carried out in a manner that creates as little disruption for Elian as possible. Far from depriving Lazaro Gonzalez of his right to appeal, we have attempted to accommodate his interests in obtaining review by the Court of Appeals while assuring a prompt and orderly reunion of Elian and his father if the District Court's decision is affirmed. This assurance is consistent with federal law and normal INS procedures.

"Under federal immigration law and INS procedure, the government routinely requests written assurances that individuals paroled into the United States will comply with the terms of their parole. The simple assurance we have sought from Lazaro Gonzalez is that he will cooperate with an orderly transfer of Elian Gonzalez in the event of an adverse ruling by the U.S. Court of Appeals and barring emergency injunctive relief from the Supreme Court. Lazaro Gonzalez will be meeting with INS and Justice Department officials tomorrow afternoon. We hope that, at that time, he will agree to the very reasonable conditions that we have set out as a condition of Elian's continued parole.

"From the beginning, we have been mindful of the fact that at the center of this case is a six-year-old boy who has been through a terrible ordeal. We are concerned for him and will continue to try to resolve this matter in a way that avoids additional trauma to him. It has been nearly 12 weeks since the Commissioner's decision, and four months since Elian was separated from his father and lost his mother. As District Court Judge Moore said in his ruling last week, 'Each passing day is another day lost between Juan Gonzalez and his son.'

"We continue to urge everyone involved to work together to understand, respect and uphold the bond between parent and child and the laws of the United States."

The very next day, the Immigration and Naturalization Department released another statement that read:

"U.S. DEPARTMENT OF JUSTICE
"IMMIGRATION AND NATURALIZATION SERVICE
"Washington, D.C. 20536
"STATEMENT
"March 29, 2000
"DOJ AND INS STATEMENT ON ELIAN GONZALEZ
"The Department of Justice (DOJ) and the Immigration and Naturalization Service (INS) have decided to continue discussions concerning Elian Gonzalez. The parties will meet at the Office of the U.S. Attorney in Miami at 9:30 a.m. tomorrow. The government will therefore defer revocation of Elian's parole status for a 24-hour period."

I reiterate once again that I do not have any legal expertise and reaffirm, one more time that I would not pretend to be Sherlock Holmes, however I can't help but notice a big difference in the tone of writing and meaning coming from the INS.

On March 28th:

"…"The simple assurance we have sought from Lazaro Gonzalez is that he will cooperate with an orderly transfer of Elian Gonzalez in the event of an adverse ruling by the U.S. Court of Appeals and barring emergency injunctive relief from the Supreme Court. Lazaro Gonzalez will be meeting with INS and Justice Department officials tomorrow afternoon. We hope that, at that time, he will agree to the very reasonable conditions that we have set out as a condition of Elian's continued parole."…"

The March 29th Statement reads:

"…"The government will therefore defer revocation of Elian's parole status for a 24-hour period."

On one day the INS is willing to wait for the determination of the U.S. Court of Appeals as a condition of Elian's continued parole and custody by Lazaro. So why, the very next day did the INS decide to "defer" the revocation of Elian's parole status for a 24-hour period?

This makes me wonder what could have transpired between the first statement and the second. What was the underlying factor eliciting such different INS statements?

After a little researching I found some interesting news articles published on March 30, 2000 by ABCNews.com. Read the following excerpt and maybe you will get an idea as to why the sudden change:

"The Cuban National Television informed: 'Cuban President Fidel Castro said during a live television broadcast in Havana Wednesday night (March 29, 2000) that Juan Miguel Gonzalez, the father of 6-year-old Elian Gonzalez, is ready to travel to the United States to claim his son."…"

The ABCNews.com report continues:

"…"Late Wednesday (March 29, 2000), Cuban leader Fidel Castro announced that passports and an airplane are ready for Elian's

father to fly to the U.S. if government officials will guarantee a
maximum effort to produce the boy. Castro proposed a plan to
send a group of friends and family members to accompany Elian's
father, but questions remain about whether the State Department
would allow an entourage.

"Gregory Craig was reported saying he would also apply for visas
for the rest of the Elian "support group.".…"

Did it really take almost four months for the communist government to make sure Juan Miguel was absolutely clear of any wrongdo-
ing and that he was not part of a conspiracy to have his child escape in
a boat?

One hundred and twenty days to assure themselves that Juan
Miguel Gonzalez was a loyal communist as he claimed to be and he
really wanted to bring his son back to Cuba?

Castro continued all the while spouting his rhetoric from his small
but belligerent domain. He was ready to send his own 'Trojan Horse'
to the capital of the United States of America!

I honestly am not trying to influence my opinion one way or
another, but it does appear that the FOURTH scenario was already as
clear and bright as a high noon sun on a cloudless summer day!

Why was the scheduled March 29th meeting between the INS, Lazaro and his lawyers postponed to the following day? Who proposed
that postponement, Lazaro's lawyers or the INS? Following is the official statement from the DOJ and INS released on March 30th:

"Immigration and Naturalization Service
"Washington, D.C. 20536
"STATEMENT
"March 30, 2000
"DOJ and INS STATEMENT ON THE ELIAN GONZALEZ
CASE
"The Department of Justice (DOJ) and the Immigration and Nat-
uralization Service (INS) have agreed to resume discussions with
Lazaro Gonzalez and his legal counsel at 10 a.m. on Monday, April

3. In the meantime, Elian's parole status will continue unchanged, and he will be allowed to remain in Lazaro Gonzalez' care. Elian's parole is therefore extended until 9 am, Tuesday, April 4.

"All parties are monitoring developments concerning the possible arrival of Juan Miguel Gonzalez in the United States.

"The Department of Justice and the INS have approached these discussions in good faith, and we hope to continue to move forward on Monday. We continue to urge the community to recognize the importance of the bond between parent and child as well as the need to uphold the laws of the United States."

We must remember that Juan Miguel Gonzalez wanted his son back and his wishes were supported by the decision of the Immigration and Naturalization Service and the Department of Justice with the ratification of U.S. Circuit Judge Moore by his ruling. We cannot ignore the collaboration of the National Council of Churches, the General Board of Church and Society of The United Methodist Church, Representative Maxine Waters and others.

And, let us not forget that while Juan Miguel Gonzalez was still in Cuba he had an American attorney in the United States overseeing and taking care of his legal rights and requests. Before Juan Miguel's arrival, Gregory Craig acted as his spokesman and as a public relations agent for his Cuban client.

Read further from the same article of ABCNews.com of March 30, 2000:

"..."Earlier in Washington, attorney Gregory Craig said he was submitting visa applications for Elian's father Juan Miguel Gonzalez, his wife and other family members for travel to the United States."

"..."Craig also demanded today a guarantee that Elian's father could take his son into custody if he made the trip and called the government's dealing with the Miami family "a failure."

"..."The relatives in Miami do not speak for Elian, the lawyers in Miami do not speak for Elian," Craig said, "The only person that has the legal and moral authority to speak for Elian Gonzalez is his father," who is ready to leave Cuba at "a moment's notice," he said."…"

President Clinton had kept silent and apparently passive in the handling and processing of Elian's case. He was leaving the details to Attorney General Reno.

Was a call placed to the White House at any time with the breaking news of Juan Miguel's forthcoming trip to Washington, D.C?

Hard to say, but what prompted First Lady Hillary Rodham Clinton to make her opinion known about this controversial case?

On April 1, 2000, Maria F. Durand reported through ABC-News.com:

> "Hillary Rodham Clinton jumped into the Elian Gonzalez controversy today, saying she opposes making him a permanent resident of the United States.
> "In a statement released by her office, the first lady said she opposed congressional action, placing herself at odds with Vice President Al Gore. "Hillary Clinton knows that we must take politics out of this decision," said Clinton Senate campaign spokesman Howard Wolfson. "Elian's future should be determined as quickly as possible through the appropriate, ongoing legal process."…"

You don't need to be Sherlock Holmes to realize the tremendous pressure that was placed over the INS and the Department of Justice to transfer the custody of Elian from his great-uncle Lazaro to his father upon Juan Miguel's arrival in Washington, D.C.

Even with Juan Miguel not yet in the United States, the INS kept pushing the subject through talks and news releases. The following statement was released:

> "U.S. DEPARTMENT OF JUSTICE
> "IMMIGRATION AND NATURALIZATION SERVICE
> "Washington, D.C. 20536
> "STATEMENT

"April 3, 2000

"DISCUSSIONS IN ELIAN GONZALEZ CASE

"Discussions will resume at 10:00 a.m. Tuesday, regarding how to begin the transfer of care of Elian Gonzalez to his father, Juan Miguel Gonzalez. No final decision has been reached in this matter, but the discussions are continuing in good faith.

"The scheduled revocation of Elian's parole tomorrow has been superseded by the expected arrival of Juan Miguel Gonzalez in the United States. The Miami relatives have long said they wanted the father to come here. The father has indicated that he wants to be here with his son. Once Mr. Gonzalez arrives, the Immigration and Naturalization Service will begin transferring parole care from Lazaro Gonzalez to the boy's father. The transfer of parole custody does not mean that the child will be immediately removed from the home of his great-uncle. Instead, it is our hope to begin a smooth and orderly process that will create as little disruption as possible for Elian. We wish to add no further trauma to that which this innocent child has already endured.

"We ask everyone involved who cares about this little boy to work with us to allow these talks to go forward in an orderly and respectful way in an effort to reach a cooperative solution."

The meeting of April 4th with the INS was postponed at the request of Lazaro's lawyer until April 6, 2000 at 9:30 a.m. The same day Juan Miguel Gonzalez was supposed to arrive in Washington, D.C.!

I remember one of my favorite stories of the Bible. David challenged, fought and defeated big Goliath! Was it possible that the small David from Miami was trying to find the appropriate rock to toss at the giant from Washington?

The little southern fellow could only find tiny pebbles in the Everglades and white sand on the beaches of South Florida.

11

CASTRO ALLOWS FATHER TO LEAVE CUBA

The arrival of Juan Miguel Gonzalez, his wife Nersy Carmenate and his infant son Hianny was announced throughout the United States. This announcement was treated with the same importance as if the head of a foreign government was coming on an official trip to visit the President of the United States in Washington, D.C.

On April 5, 2000 ABCNews.com reported:

> "…"An American lawyer representing Juan Miguel Gonzalez said he was coming with the expectation that the U.S. government would begin procedures to transfer custody to him.".…"
>
> "…Gregory Craig, a prominent American lawyer who has represented President Clinton, met with Gonzalez in Cuba earlier today. Craig flew back to Washington tonight and at a short press conference announced Gonzalez's decision.".…"
>
> "…Craig said Gonzalez decided to make the trip after the Immigration and Naturalization Service issued a statement that said: "Once Mr. Gonzalez arrives in the United States, the INS will begin transferring parole care from Lazaro Gonzalez to the boy's father.".…"

Juan Miguel Gonzalez had "decided" to come for his son 132 days after he first demanded Elian's return on November 27, 1999.

A long period of time–114 days since the INS had ruled that father and son should be reunited on January 14, 2000.

As expected, Juan Miguel, his wife and infant son arrived to Dulles International Airport, outside of Washington, D.C. in the early hours of April 6, 2000. It was exactly 139 days since he last saw Elian in Cardenas, on November 21, 1999.

I copy some excerpts from the report by ABCNews.com covering the arrival:

> "…"I believe that reuniting Elian with his father is not only a matter of federal law, it is not a matter of immigration law. It is simply the right thing to do," said Deputy Attorney General Eric Holder."…"
>
> "…"I appeal to U.S. authorities to have my son returned to me," Gonzalez said, while expressing gratitude to average Americans, who he said have been in favor of his reunification with his son. Gonzalez also thanked the psychologists and doctors in Cuba who helped him cope with the ordeal and went on to praise Fidel Castro, the "leader of my country that as a friend or brother has been next to me, advising me and supporting me in these days of pain and uncertainty."…"

After making his statements and answering questions through an interpreter, Juan Miguel, Nersey and baby Hianny went to the house of Fernando Ramirez, the head of the Cuban Interests Section in Washington, D.C. Mr. Ramirez's home was located in Bethesa, Md.

Shortly after Juan Miguel's arrival in Washington, D.C., the Department of Justice released the following Statement:

> "FOR IMMEDIATE RELEASE
> "DAG
> "THURSDAY, APRIL 6, 2000
> "(202) 616-2777
> "**WWW.USDOJ.GOV**
> "TDD (202 514-1888
> "STATEMENT OF DEPUTY ATTORNEY GENERAL ERIC HOLDER, JR., ON THE ARRIVAL OF JUAN MIGUEL GONZALEZ

"A short time ago, Elian's father, Juan Miguel Gonzalez, arrived here in the United States. He came with his wife and he came with his infant son. Their arrival is a welcome development in a case that has captured everyone's attention ever since young Elian arrived to our shores.

"At the core of this case is a little boy—so young that he does not have the capacity to make legal decisions for himself. He has a father who has clearly enjoyed a close and continuous relationship with Elian from the moment he was born. And he also has relatives in Miami who undoubtedly care deeply for this little boy.

"There have been some who have claimed that the government has acted in a heavy handed manner. I reject this notion. In January, the INS decided—and we agreed—that only Juan Miguel has the authority to speak on his son's behalf regarding immigration matters. Mr. Gonzalez has clearly and sincerely stated that he wants to be reunited with his son.

"In an effort to be fair and most importantly to consider young Elian's well-being, we did not immediately implement our decision—even though we had the authority to do so. Instead, we urged the Miami relatives to work out a cooperative arrangement to reunite Elian in a manner that was least disruptive to everyone involved.

"Since then, a federal court has upheld our decision. Then, demonstrating further restraint, we offered the Miami relatives an opportunity to appeal the court's ruling so long as they did not assure further open-ended delays.

"Today we are as committed as ever to reuniting the two in a manner that is most sensitive to Elian's well-being. This morning we will continue discussing these issues with the lawyers for the relatives in Miami. We strongly believe that Juan Miguel Gonzalez's presence here will move the process forward and will allow the parties to quickly effectuate a transfer of Elian to his father.

"I have a six year old daughter. And as a father, I cannot imagine the anguish of being separated from my daughter due to circumstances beyond my control. That is one reason that I believe reuniting Elian with his father is not only a matter of federal law, it is not a matter of immigration law. It is simply the right thing to do.

"This father and his son need to be together. And in the coming

days we will do all that we can to ensure that happens."
00-178

◆   ◆   ◆

Evidently the postponed meeting between the officials of the Immigration and Naturalization Service, the Department of Justice and the lawyers of Lazaro Gonzalez took place during the morning hours of April 6, 2000. Later that day the INS released the following statement:

"U.S. DEPARTMENT OF JUSTICE
"IMMIGRATION AND NATURALIZATION SERVICE
"Washington, D.C. 20536
"STATEMENT
"April 6, 2000
"STATEMENT OF THE DEPARTMENT OF JUSTICE
AND IMMIGRATION AND NATURALIZATION SERVICE

"We are very disappointed that, after several days of meetings, the Miami relatives of Elian Gonzalez continue to refuse to return Elian to his father, Juan Miguel Gonzalez.
"Officials from the Department of Justice and the Immigration and Naturalization Service had extended their discussions with the relatives' attorneys and deferred revocation of Elian's parole status for a week in an effort to reach a cooperative solution.
"Recognizing how much Lazaro Gonzalez and his family care for this child, we had hoped that the relatives would understand the importance of reuniting Elian and his father, with as little continued disruption.
"Unfortunately, the extended discussions did not result in assurances from the relatives that they would voluntarily transfer custody of Elian. These standard assurances are required by federal law as a condition of parole. Instead, the attorneys continued to revisit the issue of whether Elian should be reunited with his father, as opposed to discussing how best to reunite them.
"In January, the INS ruled, and the Attorney General affirmed,

that the father speaks for the son. For the past four months, Juan Miguel Gonzalez has made it very clear that he wants to be reunited with his six-year-old son. Last month, a federal court sustained the decision of the Commissioner of the INS and the Attorney General. At any point along the way, the INS and the Department of Justice could have implemented the ruling immediately, but instead we went to extraordinary lengths to try to resolve this matter in a cooperative manner.

"We will soon provide the relatives in Miami with a letter setting forth the process for reuniting Elian with his father, who arrived in the United States earlier this morning. We still hope for an orderly process for reuniting Elian with his father."

On April 7, 2000, Juan Miguel Gonzalez, accompanied by his family and his lawyer, Gregory Craig, went to a meeting with officials of the United States government in Washington, D.C. It can be assumed, without any doubt, that Juan Miguel and Gregory Craig made a firm and vehement demand that Elian be returned to his father without any further delay.

In the meantime, Lazaro and his family in Miami steadfastly remained in their position that before releasing Elian to the INS or the Department of Justice and consequently to his father, they wanted to have a face-to-face meeting with Juan Miguel.

I can't help but remember the trip of Juan Miguel's mother Mariela Quintana and his ex-mother-in-law Raquel Rodriguez. According to Mr. Edgar they were "dissuaded and frightened from visiting the Miami relatives' home."

No chance could exist that Juan Miguel was allowed by Fidel Castro to attend a get-together with any relatives living in "imperialist territory" and listen to the pleas and arguments from his GUSANO uncle in Miami.

Juan Miguel Gonzalez had no authorization or intention to meet with his uncle and family.

The statement released by Attorney General Reno summarized what was discussed during that meeting, plus a lengthy attempt to explain and justify the actions and decisions of the Immigration and Naturalization Service and the Department of Justice from November 25, 1999 through April 7, 2000.

After I retrieved this Statement through the Internet, I read it several times and I must state that each time I read it I became more perplexed over the context of this document. I must warn you that it is a long reading, but it is worth every minute you spend doing that.

The copy I have has the Seal of the Department of Justice printed on the left top corner of the first page. You can reach it at **http:// www.usdoj.gov/opa/pr/2000/April/189ag.htm**

"FOR IMMEDIATE RELEASE
"AG
"APRIL 7, 2000
"(202) 616-2777
"**WWW.USDOJ.GOV**
"TDD (202) 514-1888
"STATEMENT OF ATTORNEY GENERAL RENO
"Today, I met with Elian's father, Juan Miguel Gonzalez—a man who expressed in a very clear and a very heartfelt manner his sincere desire to have his son returned to him as soon as possible. He obviously loves Elian very much. All you had to do is look at him, and see him, to see how much he loves this little boy.
"The meeting was only with a very small group of people. Mr. Gonzalez was joined by his wife and their 6-month-old baby boy and his lawyer, Gregory Craig. I was joined by INS Commissioner Doris Meissner, Deputy Attorney General Eric Holder, a member of his staff, and an official U.S. government translator. No Cuban officials were present.
"During the hour-long meeting, Mr. Gonzalez and I had a very open and honest discussion. Throughout, he repeated what he has said time and time again—he wants his son back.
"Four months ago, Elian Gonzalez came to our shores after his mother perished at sea. While his immigration status was being resolved, he was placed in the temporary care of his great uncle who lives in Miami. As with any similar arrangement, Elian's temporary custody was conditioned on the understanding that the care-pro-

viders will abide by the instructions of the Immigration and Naturalization Service.

"In December, INS officials—on two separate occasions—interviewed Mr. Gonzalez in Cuba. Again, no Cuban officials were present. Both times, Mr. Gonzalez asserted his plea to have his child returned to him—and he said he had no desire to live in the United States.

"I wholeheartedly reject Cuba's system of government. Mr. Gonzalez and I do not share the same political beliefs.

"But it is not our place to punish a father for his political beliefs or for where he wants to raise his child. Indeed, if we were to start judging parents on the basis of their political beliefs, we would change the concept of family for the rest of time.

"After meeting with Mr. Gonzalez in Cuba, INS officials also met with relatives in Miami. We wanted to give the relatives an opportunity to provide any information they could that could be relevant to the decision.

"In January, after the interviews, the INS Commissioner announced her decision that, not only did the father speak for the son, but that the father's wishes were indeed to have his son with him.

"From that moment, nothing prevented the United States government from immediately taking action to reunite the father and son. There was no court order. No stay. No injunction. But instead of moving hastily, we gave the relatives in Miami a chance to challenge our decision in federal court. A federal court sustained our judgement, stating 'each passing day is another day lost between Juan Gonzalez and his son.'

"Thereafter, we again remained willing to postpone the reunion because we wanted to give the relatives every chance to argue their case in the federal appellate court. All we asked for in return was a pledge that—at the end of the day—when the appeals process had run its course, the Miami relatives would turn over Elian to his father voluntarily. They were unwilling to provide us with that assurance.

"For the past several weeks we have engaged in discussions with the relatives to try to come to a cooperative arrangement for reuniting Elian with his father. But instead of discussing how Elian should be reunited, the attorneys for the relatives continued to demand that we re-visit the issue of whether Elian should be reunited. That is not what the law provides.

"It has been nearly twelve weeks since the Commissioner's decision, and four months since Elian was found at sea. It is time for this little boy, who has been through so much, to be with his father. The relatives say it would be wrenching to take him from the home. Four months is no substitute for six years for a father who has had such an important role in raising such a wonderful boy.

"The law is very clear. Clearly, a child who has lost his mother belongs with his sole surviving parent, especially one with whom the child has shared such a close and continuous relationship with his son.

"I understand and respect with all my heart the deep-seated beliefs which the Cuban exile community feels on this subject. Cuba is a repressive society. A society ruled by a dictator from whom thousands have fled. Over the past four decades, Cubans have come to the United States to seek freedom and to seek a better way of life. As a result, Miami has prospered and grown. It is a wonderful city which I love very, very much.

"I know most people within the Cuban community [who] differ with my decision [...] have the best interest of Elian at heart. Many of them risked their lives to come to this country. They want him to have the opportunity that they have had. But in the end I believe that they also understand that this is a nation of laws by which all must abide. And it is a nation whose law and foundation recognize that there is a bond, a special, wonderful, sacred bond between a father and a son-one that I intend to uphold.

"Yesterday, Mr. Gonzalez came to our country to be reunited with his son. Today, we move forward with that reunification.

"Early next week, we will give instructions to the relatives on when and where Elian is to be turned over to his father. And at that time, the INS will formally transfer parole care to the father.

"By letter today we are asking the relatives to meet on Monday with two eminent psychiatrist and a distinguished psychologist to determine how the transfer can take place with as little disruption for Elian as possible. The three experts have informed us that the best way to proceed is to effect the reunification promptly. Monday's consultation will assist us, not in determining whether the transfer should occur, but how it will occur to cause the least disruption possible.

"I have been in California, in Chicago, in Chile, in Costa Rica, in these past four months. I have been in my own home town and I have been in Washington. This case has struck the heart and soul of the world.

"I urge everybody involved to move forward to effect this reconciliation and reunification as soon as possible. Elian deserves the very, very best and the best we can give him for he has been through so much. In his own way, rather than tear us apart, he has brought us together to understand the strength of the human spirit. Let us not disappoint him."

**The bracketed changes reflect the sentence as written, not as read.

00-189

◆   ◆   ◆

After I copied the text of this Statement I took my time to analyze, in depth, its content. My feelings turned from curiosity to anguish and then it burst into anger. I will not let my personal opinion influence the questions that will follow.

Can anyone believe that Juan Miguel was allowed to come to the United States without Castro being absolutely convinced that he was a loyal follower of the communist doctrine? Or at least, that they were holding something in Cuba that would deter him from changing his mind and stay in the United States with his new wife and sons?

The statement from Attorney General Reno that "No Cuban officials were present" should not be considered of importance to that meeting.

"..."In December, INS officials—on two separate occasions—interviewed Mr. Gonzalez in Cuba. Again, no Cuban offi-

cials were present. Both times, Mr. Gonzalez asserted his plea to
have his child returned to him—and he said he had no desire to
live in the United States.

"…"In January, after the interviews, the INS Commissioner
announced her decision that, not only did the father speak for the
son, but that the father's wishes were indeed to have his son with
him.

"From that moment, nothing prevented the United States government from immediately taking action to reunite the father and son.
There were no court orders. No stay. No injunction."…"

The Attorney General continuously refers to the laws of the United
States that recognize and protect the "special, wonderful bond"
between father and son. Those same laws were enacted and in full force
before November 27, 1999. That's the date when Juan Miguel Gonzalez first demanded that his son be reunited with him in Cardenas,
Cuba.

Is there any article of the law referred to by Attorney General Reno
that stipulates that any United States government official or representative could apply such a law at his/her own will when such official
considered it appropriate to enforce it? If that article doesn't exist, the
Immigration and Naturalization Service and the Department of Justice
broke the law by not applying the law in due time!

From November 27, 1999 until January 5, 2000 that special, wonderful bond between father and son was completely ignored by the
INS.

The Attorney General admitted in her statement that there was not
any court order, no stay nor an injunction that legally prevented them
from reuniting father and son.

Who broke the law first by not applying it when appropriate and
necessary? Lazaro Gonzalez or the Immigration and Naturalization
Service?

Twice, on the 13th and the 31st in December of 1999, Juan Miguel
stated to the agents of the Immigration and Naturalization Service

interviewing him in Cuba that he wanted his son back. Why didn't the INS enforce the laws of the United States and send Elian back to his father, as he had demanded?

Lazaro Gonzalez was accused of breaking the 'rule of law' of the United States. Lazaro didn't force his way into Hollywood Memorial Hospital and kidnap Elian. The INS released the boy to him on November 26, 1999!

And, from the beginning of this affair Lazaro was only trying to keep his great-nephew in a free country to honor the wishes of Elian's mother. He wanted to give Elian the opportunity to live in a free society, in the United States of America.

Attorney General Reno, better than anyone else stated the reason for those efforts from Elian's great-uncle. She wrote in her Statement:

> "…"I understand and respect with all my heart the deep-seated beliefs which the Cuban exile community feels on this subject. Cuba is a repressive society. A society ruled by a dictator from whom thousands have fled. Over the past four decades, Cubans have come to the United States to seek freedom and to seek a better way of life. As a result, Miami has prospered and grown.
> "…"I know most people within the Cuban community who differ with my decision have the best interest of Elian at heart. Many of them risked their lives to come to this country. They want him to have the opportunity that they have had. But in the end I believe that they also understand that this is a nation of laws by which all must abide."…"

I have many more questions regarding the statement of Attorney General Reno, but some are too harsh and others too painful, opinionated and close to my heart.

Again, it is not my intention to impose my personal views on you. You can read her Statement again and please, read between lines. After reading the preceding chapters of this book I believe you might have reached new conclusions and have a different opinion about this sad affair.

12

LAZARO MUST RETURN ELIAN TO INS

The actions that took place after Juan Miguel Gonzalez arrived to the United States should be considered very important. All of the different events determined the development of Elian's custody case.

I hope this is not construed derogatory by any means, but the only way I can refer to the situation at hand in April of 2000 is by comparing it to a 'five-ring' circus.

The 'main ring' was set in Miami, Florida. There Lazaro Gonzalez and his lawyers were involved in their continuing legal battle to keep Elian in the United States, and they were in constant communication with the Immigration and Naturalization Service and its officials from the Miami District office.

In Atlanta, Georgia, the U.S. Court of Appeals for the Eleventh Circuit had their hands full with the review of the appeal to the ruling of U.S. District Court Judge Moore.

In Washington, D.C., the lawyers of the INS and the Department of Justice were looking for the formula to terminate Lazaro's custody of Elian, the transfer of the boy to his father and the hope that very soon the father, son and their complete entourage would leave the United States.

In Bethesa, Maryland, while living at the home of Fernando Ramirez, Juan Miguel and his family were experiencing the style of living of the Cuban representatives in Washington, D.C. The abundance of food, the elegance of clothing, the comforts of the housing and the use of new cars must have had Juan Miguel thinking about the offers he had received to stay in the United States with his family. The legal representation and advice of his lawyer, Gregory Craig, was always at hand.

We can't forget that while all those events were occurring in the United States, Castro in Cuba continued to lift up the spirit of his followers with daily speeches and demonstrations. The chanting: FREE ELIAN...FREE ELIAN...was continuously echoing across the entire island.

This period of time must have been a nightmare for the news reporters trying to cover the latest happening in this case. It must be added that they did have a very comprehensive account of the drama as it developed.

The Immigration and Naturalization Service released the following statement on April 10, 2000:

> "U.S. DEPARTMENT OF JUSTICE
> "IMMIGRATION AND NATURALIZATION SERVICE
> "Washington, D.C. 20536
> "STATEMENT
> "April 10, 2000
> "DOJ/INS STATEMENT ON THE ELIAN GONZALEZ CASE
> "The meeting between Elian's Miami relatives and the three experts in child psychiatry and psychology has concluded. Based on the doctors' meeting yesterday with Elian's father, Juan Miguel Gonzalez, and their meeting today with Elian's Miami relatives, the doctors will soon be consulting with the Immigration and Naturalization Service (INS) on the most appropriate way to proceed with Elian's reunion with his father.
> "These consultations will serve to inform INS' decision on the best way to proceed in reuniting Elian with his father in a way that is the least disruptive to Elian. Subsequently, INS will give instructions to the Miami family on how this transfer will occur. We continue to believe that Elian's well being is best served if the Miami relatives participate in an active and responsible way in preparing Elian prior to the transfer, as well as in supporting him during and

after he is reunited with his father.

"Elian and his father, Juan Miguel, have been separated for more than four months. We hope that Elian's Miami relatives and everyone involved with this little boy will be supportive of him and his father during this time."

On April 11, 2000 Attorney General Reno and INS Commissioner Doris Meissner had a meeting in Miami with the mayors of Miami-Dade County and the City of Miami, trying to coordinate the oncoming action of reuniting father and son.

The following was a news release from the Attorney General's office:

"FOR IMMEDIATE RELEASE
"AG
"Tuesday, April 11, 2000
"(202) 616-2777
"**WWW.USDOJ.GOV**
"TDD (202) 514-1888
"STATEMENT BY ATTORNEY GENERAL JANET RENO FOLLOWING MEETING WITH MAYORS OF MIAMI
"Attorney General Janet Reno and INS Commissioner Doris Meissner met today with Miami-Dade County Mayor Alex Penelas and Miami City Mayor Joe Carollo. The Attorney General issued the following statement:
"The meeting with Mayors Penelas and Carollo was productive and I welcome their suggestions on how we can best achieve an orderly reunification of Elian with his father.
"We all agreed that helping to bring the family together to work out this orderly transition would be desirable, but I also stressed that the transfer of Elian to the care of his father must move forward without delay.
"The mayors have asked me to speak with leaders of the Miami community and I have indicated my willingness and desire to do so.
"We agreed to continue working together to seek an outcome that allows Elian to be reunited with his father in the best way possi-

ble—for him, for his family, and for the Miami community as a whole."

You can go back and read in Chapter Six again and compare the context of the previous Statement with the thinking of the southern mayors. The ideas and situations are close, but they were not the same.

General Attorney Reno warned Lazaro Gonzalez in her Statement of April 7th that she will give him instructions "on when and where" Elian was to be turned over to his father.

The Immigration and Naturalization Service sent the following letter to Lazaro Gonzalez:

"April 12, 2000

"Dear Mr. Gonzalez:

"The goal of the Department of Justice and the Immigration and Naturalization Service is to ensure that Elian's transition to his father's care is as peaceful as possible. We must all do everything in our power to see that the transfer is accomplished in a thoughtful, constructive manner.

"We understand from your attorneys and various other representatives that you would like an opportunity to meet with Juan Miguel Gonzalez. We are prepared to accommodate that request as part of an orderly transfer of the care of Elian to his father.

"To that end, please present Elian at Opa-Locka Airport, 1500 N.W. 42nd Ave., Opa-Locka, Fla., where you should proceed to the Main Coast Guard Gate at 2 p.m. Thursday, April 13. Rosa R. Urquiola, a bilingual INS official experienced in immigration matters involving children, will be there to accompany you, Elian, your daughter Marisleysis, and an agreed number of other members of your family to Washington, D.C., for this meeting. Before the meeting, Juan Miguel Gonzalez will have an opportunity to meet privately with his son. During the meeting, Elian will remain with Ms. Urquiola, and INS will have custody and care of Elian during that time. After the meeting, care and parole of Elian will be transferred to Juan Miguel Gonzalez. These successive transfers of parole and care are being ordered pursuant to 8 C.F.R. 212.5,235.2,236.3 (1999).

"If you do not wish to meet with Juan Miguel Gonzalez as described above, District Director Bob Wallis and I hereby instruct you to present Elian at the same time and place, i.e., the Main Coast Guard Gate at Opa-Locka Airport, at 2 p.m. on Thursday, April 13. At that time, the parole of Elian into your care will be revoked, and care of Elian will be temporarily transferred to Ms. Urquiola, who will bring Elian to Washington, D.C. Once Elian has arrived in Washington, D.C., he will be paroled into the care of his father. These successive transfers of parole and care are being ordered pursuant to 8 C.F.R. 212.5,235.2,236.3 (1999).

"You and your representatives have frequently stated in the last several weeks that while you did not agree with the Department of Justice's determination in this case or the federal judge's ruling upholding it, you would nevertheless abide by the law. The time has now come to carry through on that commitment, above all for the sake of a boy who deserves to have his reunion with his father take place without any further conflict or stress.

"Please contact Mr. Wallis with your response to this letter.

"Sincerely,

"Michael A. Pearson,
Executive Associate Commissioner for Field Operations"

In hindsight, it seems that Lazaro's answer to Michael Pearson's letter could have been similar to the one given by Brigadier General Anthony C. McAuliffe on December 22, 1944. The American commanding officer of the troops defending Bastogne (Battle of the Bulge) responded "NUTS" when General Fritz Bayerlein requested the surrender of that city to the attacking German army.

On April 13, 2000, Attorney General Reno kept her promise to mayors Penelas and Carollo. She released two Statements through the Department of Justice information system: One was to inform the whole nation about the current status of the Elian's case and the other directed to the 'people of Miami.'

I don't know exactly how the official, informative statements and press releases from the INS and the Department of Justice were supposed to reach the people on the street.

How many statements or press releases from the Department of Justice did you read, or even hear of, prior to reading them in the pages of this book?

Through the Internet I was able to research and retrieve every one of the statements I have been quoting from. I wonder how many of the Cuban exiles they wanted to reach in this case had access to a PC? I don't recall of any of these informative documents ever being read in their entirety by an anchorperson on any of the morning, afternoon, or evening television or radio news programs.

Could it be that the statements were written and released in order to keep some type of record, such as a diary of the events as they developed?

Here is another such statement:

"FOR IMMEDIATE REALESE
"AG
"THURSDAY, APRIL 13, 2000
"(202) 616-2777
"**WWW.USDOJ.GOV**
"TDD (202) 514-1888
"STATEMENT OF ATTORNEY GENERAL JANET RENO
"Good evening. For the last six weeks, we have worked hard to bring the family together with the hope that the family itself could work out a cooperative agreement. Unfortunately, although still possible, that agreement remains elusive.

"An agreement among the family members would by far and away the best solution. It is still a possibility, and we urge all concerned to pursue the possibility. But, it is not in the interest of anyone, least of all Elian, to let this matter drag on.

"Commissioner Meissner and I flew to Miami today to do everything possible to resolve this matter in the way least damaging to the child. To this end, we developed a plan in consultation with two child psychiatrists and a child psychologist. Over the past four days these experts met separately with Juan Miguel and Lazaro Gonzalez. Their objective was to determine, not whether, but how best to reunite Elian with his father in the least disruptive manner possible.

"They provided us with excellent guidance. And I am very grateful to them.

"First, the three experts believe that reunification should take place as soon after the father's arrival in this country, as possible. That is why we asked that Elian be reunited just one week after Mr. Gonzalez arrived here.

"Secondly, they feel it would be best if the reunification took place at a neutral location—away from the protesters and cameras. That is why we have secured a neutral retreat site near Washington, DC, where the family can meet away from the glare of the media, the public and Cuban government officials.

"And third, they believe it would be best for Elian if either Lazaro Gonzalez, his great uncle, or his cousin, Marisleysis, were present. That is why our letter asks that either— or both—of these care givers travel to the retreat site with Elian and be at his side when he is reunited with his father. This will also give the relatives an opportunity to meet privately with Juan Miguel Gonzalez prior to Elian's transfer to his father's care.

"We have provided the relatives and Elian the opportunity to travel to Washington, DC area and meet with Juan Miguel and participate in an orderly transfer. If not, we have provided them alternative instructions that call for them to bring Elian to the Opa-Locka Airport tomorrow afternoon, where his care will be transferred and he will be flown to the Washington area site to be reunited with his father.

"I think it is obvious and I believe Mr. Lazaro Gonzalez and his daughter care deeply about Elian. I truly believe that. Since his arrival in the United States they have served as loving caregivers. It is now up to them to ensure that Elian's transition from their care to the care of his father, Juan Miguel Gonzalez, happens in the best and least traumatic way.

"As I have said before, this case is about a father and his son. It is a bond that is recognized in the law—and appreciated by every parent around the world. Although Juan Miguel Gonzalez has been separated from his son for four long months, his bond with Elian has never—ever been severed. I know that because I met with Mr. Gonzalez—a man who helped raise Elian and make him into the fine young boy he is today. And without any Cuban officials present, I heard his plea in his own words. He loves his son and he wants him back.

"In this last week I have heard so many, reaffirming their faith in the rule of law in this nation. Everyone in this case cares deeply about a remarkable 6-year-old boy. A little boy that defines the strength and courage of the human spirit. In the coming days, I urge everyone concerned to think of Elian and to respect the rule of law. Let us make this community a model for what Castro's Cuba is not. Let us make this community a community where people can speak freely without violence and with respect for each other. Let us not disappoint Elian. Let us come together and let us work a way that will best protect the rule of law and this little boy. Thank you."

00-203

I could make many comments regarding the contents of Statement 00-203 from Attorney General Reno but that would be very opinion-ated on my side and give you my personal point of view in this matter. I will restrain myself to just a couple of remarks.

Thursday, April 13, 2000 is the date of Statement 00-203. The date of this Statement could be an honest mistake, or maybe it was released to the public one day too late. By the time this Statement was printed FOR IMMEDIATE RELEASE, Lazaro Gonzalez should have surren-dered Elian to the custody of the INS official Rosa R. Urquiola, at Opa-Locka Airport at 2 p.m. Those were the instructions contained in the letter dated April 12, 2000 from Michael A. Pearson, Executive Associate Commissioner for Field Operations of the INS to Lazaro Gonzalez. (See paragraph #8 of Statement 00-203)

The meaning of the first paragraph of that Statement is open to interpretation, because everyone was already fully aware of the efforts of the Immigration and Naturalization Service and the Department of Justice towards the reunification of Elian and his father.

You must remember that Juan Miguel Gonzalez was physically present in the United States since the early hours of April 6, 2000 only after the Cuban communist government allowed him to fly to Washington, D.C.

Maybe you can understand the first paragraph of this Statement but it is a bit confusing to me:

> "Good evening. For the last six weeks, we have worked hard to bring the family together with the hope that the family itself could work out a cooperative agreement."

Well, you can hear a story so many times that it's possible you end-up believing it!

Yes, I believe that Cuban officials were NOT present during the meeting between the Attorney General, and Juan Miguel and his American lawyer. Yes, I accept the affirmation that NO communist authorities were in the same room when the INS interviewed the father twice in Cuba.

But it will be extremely hard to convince me that Juan Miguel Gonzalez was not under the full control of the Cuban authorities at home and while abroad.

Do you remember the comments of Mr. Edgar from the National Council of Churches? In Miami Beach he told Sister O'Laughlin that he felt "Castro himself was calling the shots. Cuban officials" he continued, "dissuaded and frightened the grandmothers from visiting the Miami relatives' home."

I have no doubt that Juan Miguel loved Elian and he wanted him back! But you and I only need to hear, directly from Juan Miguel himself, his statement upon his arrival to Dulles Airport in Washington, D.C. Among other things he went on, in his own words:

> "...To praise Fidel Castro, the leader of my country that as a friend or brother has been next to me, advising me and supporting me in these days of pain and uncertainty."

Was there any reason for a representative of the Cuban communist government to be present when Juan Miguel Gonzalez spoke to the officials of the government of the United States?

What do you think, Dr. Watson? Do we need more evidence in this case?

13

ATTORNEY GENERAL UNDER FIRE

The only way I can describe the tension in Little Havana on the morning of April 13, 2000 is like the humming of a high voltage electric transmission line. The previous day's ultimatum from the Immigration and Naturalization Service to deliver Elian to them by 2.00 p.m. had many ears and eyes listening to or watching continuous reports by radio and television stations.

In a lighthearted manner we can consider the following scene as a fair description of the events expected to climax that afternoon at the Opa-Locka Airport located approximately 12 miles north of Lazaro's home.

Across the whole arena the voice of the announcer echoes before a highly publicized boxing match between two world champions:

> 'In this corner we have the smaller but certainly feisty Bantamweight Champion of the World, weighing 118 pounds. He's challenging the taller, and much bigger, belt holder of the Heavyweight division, who is standing in the other corner and weighing in at 220 pounds of muscle and bones.'

It promised to be an extremely tense day for everyone involved in the Elian Gonzalez affair.

Before going into the description of what actually happened, I want to copy the Statement dated April 13, 2000 released by the Department of Justice in which Attorney General Reno apparently tried to reach the people in Miami.

"FOR IMMEDIATE RELEASE
"AG
"THURSDAY, APRIL 13, 2000
"(202) 616-2777
"**WWW.USDOJ.GOV**
"TDD (202) 514-1888
"STATEMENT OF ATTORNEY GENERAL JANET RENO
"I want to talk to the people of Miami directly today to explain the efforts to resolve the Elian Gonzalez matter and to address the mis-understandings that sometimes exist in a terribly tense situation such as this.

"Elian's Miami relatives have asked to meet privately with Juan Miguel Gonzalez, his father, to have the chance to try to convince him that Elian should stay here, and barring that, to at least reas-sure themselves that he is truly speaking for himself. We have arranged an opportunity for such a meeting—and that opportunity still exists.

"As I stated last night in my meeting with Elian's Miami relatives, as well as in our letter to Mr. Lazaro Gonzalez, and in my state-ment to the press, we have made arrangements for Lazaro Gonzalez and his family to be flown to Washington, DC—at no expense to themselves—to meet with Juan Miguel privately.

"This meeting would take place before Elian is transferred to his father's care. It would take place at a private retreat site where this family can finally sit down face-to-face and try to work things out among themselves. If they could work things out amongst them-selves, the government would step aside. But if, at the end of the day they could not reach an agreement, the relatives would abide by the rule of law.

"We stand by this offer and Juan Miguel Gonzalez has agreed to participate. Unfortunately, Lazaro Gonzalez and his family have refused these arrangements.

"Secondly, another rumor that exists is that the government is "fed-eralizing" the streets around Lazaro Gonzalez' home and ejecting the media. These rumors are wrong, flat out wrong. We have not taken any such steps and have no plans to do so. I can also assure the public that they will not see Marshals at 2:01 today attempting to remove the child by force.

"I am prepared to enforce the law. But I want to be clear that if we are compelled to enforce our order, we intend to do so in a reasonable, measured way—the approach that we have always taken in this matter.

"We have the authority to take action, but responsible authority means not only being able to take action—but knowing when and how to take that action.

"Finally, the lawyers for Elian's relatives have informed us that they may be filing for a temporary injunction with the 11th Circuit Court of Appeals. Our attorney will review that motion and respond appropriately in court.

"Despite all the tension, it was wonderful to look out the window this morning and to see this beautiful city lying beyond the bay, to look to the west towards the everglades, to look to the Spanish tiles on the roof of the Federal building, to realize that this community represents America and all that it is about. It represents America and the people who have come to this land for freedom, for opportunity, for the right to speak their mind free of violence. It is a great community and a community that if we come together in this time of tension where people obviously disagree with tremendous emotion, but if we come together, if we respect each other, if we respect the rule of law, we can work through it."
00-205

Again, while I have several comments I would like to make regarding the aforementioned Statement 00-205, I will refrain from making them. After reading the Statement and knowing what happened a few days later it would not be very difficult for me to ask many questions about its contents, but unfortunately they wouldn't be from an objective point of view.

I would like to only ask: Did Attorney General Reno have any advance information regarding what Lazaro Gonzalez would do that afternoon, at 2.00 p.m.? She seemed to have the answers before the questions were asked...

On April 13, 2000 television viewers such as myself who followed the tug-of-war between Lazaro and his nephew Juan Miguel woke to the viewing of a homemade video on the news that we were not expecting to see.

ABCNews.com gave the Spanish-language television channel, Univision, credit for the exclusive broadcast of the Elian family-made videotape. Evidently there was some arrangement between the broadcasters. Even though I live out of the range of Univision, I watched on the early morning news as Elian, pointing at the camera, broadcasted to the world in Spanish his feelings concerning his repatriation to Cuba.

Elian was telling his father that he wanted to stay in the United States. He told Juan Miguel that if he wanted he could stay here with him, and Elian repeated that he did not want to go back to Cuba.

One thing was clear, although in a few different words; Elian repeated the same statement he had made after visiting with his grandmothers. He clearly repeated that he did not want to go back to Cuba.

Did you see that videotape? What do you think? Was Elian telling his father in his own words that they must stay in the United States?

Do you think he was coached? Was he told what to do, how to act in front of the camera and what to say? He pointed his right index finger at the camera while insisting on staying in Miami!

The new videotape fed into the emotions of two very opposite camps in this drama. One side believed that Elian was coached and forced to speak to his father in the way he did as captured on the videotape. The opposite side asserted that the child was talking by himself and he had expressed his own feelings without coaching or rehearsal. Many believe Elian was telling the world how he felt about being forced to return to Cardenas, Cuba.

I was not present when the video was taped, therefore, I cannot testify one way or another!

The town clock chimed twice and the magic hour of 2:00 p.m. on April 13, 2000 arrived. And it passed without Elian Gonzalez showing up at the Coast Guard's main gate at the Opa-Locka Airport.

It must have been extremely frustrating for the officials of the INS when they realized that Lazaro Gonzalez was not going to follow their clear and precise orders to bring his great-nephew to the Opa-Locka Airport to initiate his flight to Washington, D.C. to be reunited with his father.

But, Rosa R. Urquiola, Robert Wallis and Michael A. Pearson only needed to watch television at the Coast Guard station. At 2:00 p.m. Elian was featured on television shown playing in the yard of his great-uncle's home in Little Havana.

Was there any special premonition in the earlier Statement from Attorney General Reno?

I noticed two things regarding the contents of that Statement and the Attorney General was right on both counts!

The U.S. Marshals did not go to Lazaro's home at 2:01 p.m. to seize Elian and, the Miami family's lawyers had filed a motion in court which was granted: a temporary injunction by the 11th U.S. Circuit Court of Appeals. The large crowd of Cuban-Americans that had been gathering on and around Lazaro's street in Little Havana broke into a fury of rejoice and happiness in learning of the court's decision granting the temporary injunction.

Did the demonstrators realize that the injunction was only a temporary remedy to the situation? Did they know that the injunction was only to prevent Elian's removal from United States territory? Were they aware that the injunction did not prevent, stop nor prohibit the Immigration and Naturalization Service to continue in their efforts to reunite Elian with his father?

I was not in Little Havana when that situation developed, therefore I cannot testify as to what was being said there. But by the crowd's reaction, it appears the majority of Cuban-Americans congregated thought that a mayor decision was taken in favor of their cause. The

American and Cuban flags were waving more vigorously than ever before. The rosaries were depicted as an expression that their prayers were answered. The chanting and expression of happiness and thanksgiving were reflected on almost every face.

I still feel a knot in my throat every time I remember the image of an elderly Cuban man caught on camera. He was on his knees when a camera crew evidentially spotted him. I was very moved when I saw him kissing the pavement of the street where he was kneeling. I remember his face, with tears filling his eyes as he expressed his feelings, "Gracias, America! Gracias, Americanos! Gracias, America! Gracias, Americanos..." That man kept repeating his chant as the camera panned away and focused on other crowd reactions.

It might seem that I failed in my promise not to show partiality while I describe situations, but I can't help but hurt in thinking that the emotions of many passionate and innocent people were handled in such a cruel and heartless way.

What was happening in the other 'rings' while the Cuban-Americans were prematurely celebrating in Little Havana?

ABC News' correspondents Ron Claiborne in Miami and Morton Dean from Havana along with reporter Ellen Davis and writer Maria F. Durand contributed to a very comprehensive and extensive report that was published on April 13, 2000 on the Internet by ABCNews.com.

I'll copy two paragraphs of that report. It will show the attitude of the communist Cuban government toward the efforts of the Immigration and Naturalization Service and the Department of Justice to reunite Elian and Juan Miguel Gonzalez:

> "..."Miguel Alvarez, a chief aide of senior Cuban official Ricardo Alarcon, said if Juan Miguel receives his son in a peaceful way, he might remain in the United States through the appeals process. But he said if the U.S. government has to take the boy by force, then Juan Miguel would leave with the boy immediately, or as soon as he can.

"He said Juan Miguel Gonzalez's time in the United States could depend on whether the U.S. government grants visas for what the Cubans call the 'support group' of some 20 people. President Castro had wanted this larger group to accompany Juan Miguel, his wife and their baby son—Elian's stepmother and half brother—when they flew to Washington last week. The group includes at least one teacher, a mental-health professional and several of the boy's former classmates from the town of Cardenas."…"

Was Fidel Castro setting conditions, placing demands and telling the Clinton Administration what to do, how to do things and when to do it?

Do you remember the statement: "No Cuban officials were present"? Right!

What do you think? Did Cuban officials really need to be present at any of the meetings or interviews between Juan Miguel and the agents of the Immigration and Naturalization Service or the meetings with Attorney General Reno?

You can re-read the last two quoted paragraphs and reach your own conclusions! Do you have any questions or any comments you would like to make? Please, you can rest assured you're protected by the First Amendment of our Constitution to do so.

In the meantime, in the Washington, D.C. 'ring', the Department of Justice decided not to pursue, momentarily, the termination of Lazaro's custody of Elian and his reunification with his father while the court reviewed the case now in their hands.

Also from Washington, D.C., Juan Miguel's attorney Gregory Craig accused the Miami relatives of breaking the law by holding Elian against the wishes of his client. He demanded that Attorney General Reno enforce the 'rule of law' and deliver Elian to his father.

Attorney General Reno was under fire from almost every conceivable angle:

1—Castro and his communist government were shouting from Havana, and basically accusing the United States of failing to reunite Elian with Juan Miguel.

2—Gregory Craig and Juan Miguel Gonzalez were pressing the Attorney General for immediate action to consummate the reunification of father and son.

3—Lazaro Gonzalez kept the pressure on as he ignored the demand to surrender Elian to the Immigration and Naturalization Service agents until he had an opportunity to speak face to face with Juan Miguel.

4—The Cuban-American community with the support of a considerable number of Anglo Americans kept their own pressure on regarding their desire for the boy.

And last but not least, the comments that came from Attorney General Reno's own forces within the Department of Justice were unexpected.

The day after the aborted reunification attempt, April 14, 2000, ABCNews.com published a report from John Cochran:

> "…"Some officials in her own Justice Department believe she is taking the wrong course, that she should be in Washington, not Miami and that she overestimates her ability to influence the Cuban community. They say she should have moved more decisively to return Elian to his father."…"

I have heard this phrase many times from American friends: "There is nothing worse than being in the wrong place at the wrong time." I want to add myself, "And to be involved in the wrong fight."

This might be the right moment to quote the words of the 37th President of the United States:

> "The greatness comes not when things go always good for you. But the greatness comes when you're tested, when you take some knocks, some disappointments, when sadness comes. Because only

if you've been in the deepest valley can you ever know how magnificent it is to be on the highest mountain."

14

JANET RENO APPROVES RAID

Attorney General Reno and INS Commissioner Meissner returned to Washington, D.C. after a frustrating and fruitless trip to South Florida.

The compounded events of Thursday, April 13th must have had the Attorney General and the officials of the INS turning their heads in disbelief watching how their plan to reunite Elian and Juan Miguel was provisionally busted and further delayed by the temporary injunction ordered by the 11th U.S. Circuit Court of Appeals.

Lazaro's refusal to obey the direct order to bring Elian to Opa-Locka Airport and the temporary injunction preventing Elian's removal from the United States, must have had the highest officials of the Department of Justice and the INS feverishly planning what should be their next move.

The position of Attorney General of the United States requires among its obvious duties, to make appearances, deliver speeches and present awards related to its field of responsibilities and expertise. The activities programmed for the week beginning on April 17, 2000 was not different than any other one in that regard.

The programs scheduled for Wednesday, April 19, 2000 included the morning appearance of the Attorney General at the Crime Victims Service Award ceremony at the Russell Senate Office Building in Washington, D.C. Her busy schedule required the Attorney General to be in Oklahoma City that same afternoon to deliver remarks at the dedication of the Oklahoma City National Memorial.

While those events were taking place in the Washington, D.C. 'ring', the 11th U.S. Court of Appeals extended its temporary injunction of April 13, 2000.

ABCNews.com filed an extensive news report in that regard. I copy two paragraphs of that article:

> "April 19—In a major victory for Elian Gonzalez's Miami relatives, a federal appeals court panel today ordered that the boy remain in the United States while the family appeals a decision to send him back to Cuba.
>
> "Furthermore, the three-judge panel of the 11th U.S. Circuit Court of Appeals questioned the strength of the federal government's case. It said the Immigration and Naturalization Service position that Elian was unable to apply for asylum without his father's support was potentially inconsistent with federal law. The ruling was a blow to the Justice Department that had hoped the panel would order the family to quickly turn the boy over to his father, Juan Miguel Gonzalez—sparing federal authorities the unwelcome possibility of having to seize the boy.
> "The panel did not do so. In fact, it didn't comment on where in the United States the boy belongs during the appeals process"…"

Television news teams were alert and were quick to broadcast the Gonzalez family's reaction in Little Havana. Upon hearing the news, the Cuban exile crowd that congregated on 'Lazaro's street' reacted immediately expressing their happiness and great rejoice. Television screens across the nation displayed the great-uncle and Elian smiling from their home's front porch. They were waving to their supporters with obvious expressions of triumph.

That same day the Department of Justice released the following statement:

"FOR IMMEDIATE RELEASE
"AG
"WEDNESDAY, APRIL 19, 2000
"(202) 616-2777
"**WWW.USDOJ.GOV**
"TDD (202) 514-1888
"STATEMENT BY ATTORNEY GENERAL JANET RENO
"ON THE 11TH CIRCUIT COURT OF APPEALS DECISION

"For the past four months, the case of Elian Gonzalez has touched the hearts of virtually every American. It is a case about a 6-year old boy—and the sacred bond that exists between he and his father. It is that simple—Juan Miguel is in this country and wants his son back.

"I believe Elian should be reunited with his father. I have said that all along. The order today from the Court of Appeals says that Elian should not be removed from the country and we will abide by that order. But it does not disagree with my determination that the boy should be reunited with his father in the United States as soon as possible. In fact, the court said that 'we need not decide where or in whose custody Plaintiff should remain while this appeal is pending.'

"There are two issues here that must be kept separate. One is whether an asylum application can be brought by distant relatives over the objection of a father who is the sole surviving parent. The other issue is who cares for the child while he is in the United States. The appeal addresses only the asylum issue, not the care issue. The court's order does not preclude me from placing Elian in his father's care while he is in the United States.

"The immigration laws clearly call for a child to be placed in the care of a parent in preference to a more distant relative while the child's immigration status is being resolved.

"The 11th Circuit's order prevents the child from leaving the country, while the appeal is pending. We will abide by the court's order.

"We are still reviewing the court's decision as I have just had a chance to read it. And we will consider all options and take the course of action most appropriate under the circumstances."

00-220

Attorney General Reno had found the 'Achilles heel' to her problem! The three-judge panel of the 11th U.S. Circuit Court of Appeals did not rule on who should have custody of Elian, the young Plaintiff of the case under consideration.

The big problem in both the Immigration and Naturalization Service and the Department of Justice camps was that the Attorney General, the INS Commissioner, or any of their advisors had no idea or a plan as to how to exploit that weakness in Elian's custody case.

It is very easy to be critical of other people's actions or decisions, especially after the fact. Hindsight is usually more precise than intelligent foresight! But, the fact is that I am describing in this book events that happened, not trying to foresee the future.

Obviously, because of the language barrier, Juan Miguel's attorney Gregory Craig spoke to the news reporters on behalf of his client and he demanded that Attorney General Reno act immediately to finalize the reunification of father and son.

In the news article of April 13, 2000 from ABCNews.com mentioned earlier in this chapter, Gregory Craig stated:

> "…"In fact, the 11th Circuit's opinion places the obligation to act squarely on the shoulders of the Attorney General." Craig said Reno had promised the boy's father last Friday that he would soon be reunited with Elian…
> "We call upon the United States government to take immediate action. It is unconscionable to wait one day longer."

Was President Clinton informed that his friend and former attorney had asked for the United States government to take immediate action in the Elian Gonzalez case? Did the White House have any intention of intervening in this matter? Did Greg Craig really think President Clinton would get directly involved in this volatile and highly publicized drama?

Perhaps the President, looking out through the windows of the second floor of the White House, got a quick glance at the BUCK running wild through the streets of Washington, D.C. before turning tail on its way to South Florida, at full gallop...

On the afternoon of Good Friday, April 21, 2000 Attorney General Reno was in her office in Washington, D.C. and she had an emotional interview with Juan Miguel Gonzalez. I can assume that Juan Miguel went to that meeting with his attorney Gregory Craig, even if the attorney's name was not included in the statement.

> "FOR IMMEDIATE RELEASE
> "AG
> "APRIL 21, 2000
> "(202) 616-2777
> "**WWW.USDOJ.GOV**
> "TDD (202) 514-2777
> "STATEMENT BY ATTORNEY GENERAL JANET RENO ON MEETING WITH JUAN MIGUEL GONZALEZ
> "Attorney General Janet Reno met this afternoon with Juan Miguel Gonzalez. She issued the following statement:
> "I met this afternoon for the second time with Elian's father, Juan Miguel Gonzalez. He expressed his great concern for the welfare of his son and urged me to take action to reunify him with Elian.
> "I was deeply moved by Mr. Gonzalez' evident love for his son. I assured him that I would continue working toward the goal of reuniting him with his child, but I also told him that I could not commit to a particular course of action or timetable."
> 00-223

I believe this is the right time to recall my late Irish mother-in-law's wisdom. She had the perfect recommendation for situations like this one: "If you can't stand the heat, get out of the kitchen!"

It may sound sarcastic, but I must mention that the text of Statement 00-223 doesn't have any reference to the effect that 'no Cuban government officials were present.'

I will probably never know who really attended that meeting, but I can safely guess that the topics discussed that afternoon of April 21st, with who ever was present, was a lot more extensive than was reported in the Attorney General's diary-like statement.

The events that developed the next morning, between 5:14 A.M. and 5:17 A.M., on April 22, 2000, in Miami, Florida, certainly can and certainly does justify my skeptical suspicions.

While doing research on this case through the Internet I found more articles, reports and informative columns then I could read through even if I sat in front of my PC for a full year!

Very descriptive reports and journalist articles were published, reflecting opposing opinions, describing the para-military action called "Operation Reunion."

Before I make a few comments regarding that forceful action I want to copy the Attorney General's statement in her attempt to explain and justify the raid by federal armed agents on the home of Lazaro Gonzalez and his family.

"FOR IMMEDIATE
"AG
"SATURDAY, APRIL 22, 2000
"(202) 616-2777
"**WWW.USDOJ.GOV**
"TDD (202) 514-1888
"ATTORNEY GENERAL STATEMENT REGARDING
 THE REMOVAL OF ELIAN GONZALEZ
"Good morning. Earlier this morning, federal agents in Miami upheld the rule of law and began to reunite Elian Gonzalez with his father. As I speak, Elian is safe and on a plane headed from Homestead Air Force Base to Andrews Air Force Base where he will be reunited with his father for the first time in 5 months.

"When the two are reunited, they will remain together in the United States throughout the appeals process while the injunction is in place. And, in accordance with the Court of Appeals ruling, we will take every step necessary to ensure that Elian does not leave the country while the Court of Appeals injunction is in place.

"We have been to great lengths to resolve this case in the least disruptive manner possible. Up until the last [moment], we tried every way we could to encourage Lazaro Gonzalez to voluntarily hand the child over to his father.

"Unfortunately, the Miami relatives rejected our efforts—leaving us no other option but the enforcement action.

"Elian Gonzalez is a child who needs to be cherished—he needs to have quiet time, private time, to be with his father. And that is what this case is still all about—the bond between father and son. Juan Miguel Gonzalez wants to be with his son and that is what has happened now.

"More than three months ago the INS determined that only Juan Miguel Gonzalez could speak for his son on immigration matters. From that moment, I could have taken action to return Elian to his father. But I did not.

"Instead I gave the Miami relatives a chance to challenge my decision in federal district court. They did and the court sided with the government. It ruled that this was a federal case and that the INS was right to say that the father speaks for the child.

"Two weeks ago, a state family court turned away the Miami relatives as well. In a strongly worded opinion, the judge said not only that the matter belonged in federal court, but that a 6-year old boy is far too young to make life altering decisions on his own.

"The same week, I traveled to Miami to try to encourage the family members to work out a resolution. The relatives in Miami said all they wanted was a meeting with Juan Miguel Gonzalez, before turning over the child. But when I arranged that meeting, they still refused to produce Elian.

"Every step of the way the Miami relatives kept moving the goal posts and raising more hurdles.

"That is why I finally directed the relatives to turn over the child 9 days ago. That deadline carried great significance. When Lazaro Gonzalez didn't comply, parole and care was revoked. That means that for the past 9 days, Lazaro Gonzalez has not had lawful custody of Elian.

"When the INS places an unaccompanied child into the care of an adult, that adult is required to abide by the directives of the INS. To maintain—as the Miami relatives did—that the INS somehow lacks authority over the immigration parole of a minor in the U.S. simply ignores the law.

"So this morning I commenced an operation with the paramount concern being the well-being of Elian and the safety of the agents and others.

"After negotiating through the night, I informed the parties that time had run out. At that moment, I gave the go-ahead for the operation.

"After I had already set the operation in motion, the intermediaries called back to offer one more counteroffer. I indicated that I was willing to continue to engage in dialogue, but time had run out. I did until the final moments try to reach a voluntary solution. Law enforcement personnel on the scene, were authorized to, and did, make the final call as to when to enter the Gonzalez home.

"Eight agents were in the house during the operation. They were there for three minutes. During that time, a female agent picked up Elian, and spoke to him in Spanish.

"The agents then took Elian to Watson Island where they boarded a helicopter bound for Homestead Air force Base. There he was examined by a doctor to make sure there were no injuries. At that point, he was boarded onto a U.S. Marshal's plane headed to Washington DC where his father is anxiously waiting for his son.

"This has been a very emotional case for everyone involved. The most important thing is Elian is safe and that no one is seriously hurt.

"As we all await the outcome of the appellate process, I think it is important for us all to accept Elian's long over-due reunion with his father.

"It is time to heal the wounds that have divided this community that is so dear to me.

"Let us give him and his father the space, the calm and the moral support they need to reconnect and reaffirm their bond between father and son."
00-225

The "rule of law" was an expression used many times in the statements and press releases from the Department of Justice and the INS.

Would you agree that anyone who doesn't follow or obey the "rule of law" is obviously breaking it? When or if you purposely and deliberately break the law, that action makes you a lawbreaker...right? And, normally a lawbreaker is summoned, indicted and/or arrested…and needs to respond to that infraction or violation in a 'court' of law.

Any violation against the 'rule of law' must be heard, examined and sanctioned by the proper authority: a judge. At no time does the law allow any enforcement agency to proceed in a way as to unreasonably force anyone to follow the 'rule of law.' Isn't that a fact, Dr. Watson?

It is not my intention whatsoever to suggest that Lazaro, Marisleysis or any member of the Gonzalez family should have been arrested for disobeying the orders of the Immigration and Naturalization Service agents and/or ignoring the Department of Justice decrees.

But, is there any doubt in anyone's mind that before taking a forceful action to implement the 'rule of law,' the Department of Justice should have summoned the entire Gonzalez family to a 'court' of law? Shouldn't they have been given an opportunity to explain to a judge why they felt so compelled to continue ignoring the orders of the Immigration and Naturalization Service to return Elian to them?

I don't know your feelings about the drastic action taken by the Department of Justice and I would respect your opinion in that regard, but I must state that I'm still numb in remembering the scene I watched on television.

Frankly, I couldn't believe what I was seeing. I wondered who was responsible for taking me to Havana during my sleep. Foolishly, I thought that someone must have used the time machine and I was transported back to Havana, Cuba!

This must be a nightmare, oh yes…This has to be a terrible nightmare…No way—This could not be happening in the United States—I kept telling myself!

But, I was wrong about all of those thoughts. I had witnessed the developments of and end result of "Operation Reunion." And, the highest law enforcement authority of the federal government of the United States was responsible for the authorization and 'go-ahead' order!

In only three minutes of the fifth hour of April 22, 2000, the whole story of liberty and justice that we so proudly proclaim to the world was violated and ignored by the Attorney General of the United States, Janet Reno.

Throughout the pages of this book I have described how this affair was conducted up to that moment and I am not trying to change your mind if you still believe that the Attorney General conducted this whole event under the 'rule of law'.

As I've stated before, I never intended to be Sherlock Holmes or present myself as an expert in law. And, I will not be a clairvoyant either, but you can rest assured that Ms. Reno's performance will be highly scrutinized by scholars when they write about the years 1999 and 2000 in the history book of the United States of America!

I personally do not envy her legacy to our country! Yes, she will be remembered as the first female Attorney General of the United States. But, she will also be remembered as the Attorney General that tampered with the personal liberties treasured so much by the citizens of this country.

Her authorization to break into the home of a family, whose only crime was trying to keep a Cuban child in the United States and save him from the dictatorship of communism, is outrageous. I broke my promise. I really can't help but state my point of view at this time!

I did much research and found many good articles from political analysts, reporters, columnists and politicians. I could make many remarks regarding this unbelievable event but again, I will refrain from doing so.

I was very fortunate to find one very descriptive and comprehensive column written on May 2, 2000 by Deroy Murdock, a syndicated columnist and Senior Fellow with the Atlas Economic Research Foundation in Fairfax, Virginia. Most of his articles and commentary columns are published through the Scripps Howard News Service. I will quote extensively from his article:

"The Bill of Rights encompasses 10 amendments. By snatching Elian Gonzalez from his great-uncle's Little Havana home, the Clinton-Reno regime either tip-toed around or trampled at least half of these protections…

"The fact that the Department of Justice conducted this affront to American liberty is breathtaking.

"Here, in order, are the provisions of the Bill of Rights that now lie tattered on the floor:

"*The First Amendment's freedom of the press could not shield an NBC News crew from the abuses it endured during the raid. Federal agents kicked cameraman Tony Zumbado in the stomach and both yanked an audio cable from his camera and otherwise disabled his gear. He told NBC's David Bloom that the feds "put their foot on my back and told me not to move or else they were going to shoot."

Soundman Gustavo Moller was struck in the head by another officer's rifle and ordered to stay still or be shot. Moller told me he suffered a small gash, "but because it was the forehead, it was bleeding a lot."…"

"*Immigration and Naturalization Service Commissioner Doris Meissner told CBS that overwhelming force was necessary due to "the possibility that there might be guns" in the Gonzalez home. So what? The Second Amendment guarantees the right "to keep and bear arms." If the mere presence of firearms on private property justifies such federal behavior, residents of the 40 percent of American homes with guns should sleep with their eyes open."…"

"*By using an improper search warrant, the Justice Department violated Fourth Amendment restrictions against "unreasonable searches and seizures." This document was signed not during business hours by K. Michael Moore, the federal district judge hearing Elian's case, but on Good Friday at 7:20 p.m. by a magistrate unfamiliar with the matter. The warrant application claimed Elian was "a concealed person," which he wasn't, and that he is "an illegal alien," which he isn't. The affidavit also failed to mention Lazaro Gonzalez's alleged weapons that supposedly required a SWAT team's response.

"Harvard law professor Alan Dershowitz, a Clinton ally, dismisses this warrant and says the administration, "acted lawlessly." As he told Fox News: "It's a dangerous day for all Americans."

"*The Sixth Amendment includes the right to "the assistance of counsel" in criminal proceedings. Elian is no crook, but the spirit of this amendment suggests that he may see the lawyers who are arguing his asylum case. Elian's attorneys cannot contact him now, nor even observe his condition while surrounded by U.S. Marshals. "Even worse, the only lawyer in touch with Elian is Greg Craig, his father's counsel, who is working to vacate the Cuban castaway's asylum application. This is like having Leonid Brezhnev represent Alexander Solzhenitsyn in court.

"*The 10th Amendment reserves powers "to the States respectively, or to the people" that are not constitutionally delegated to the federal government. Nonetheless, Washington intervened in a child custody matter routinely handled by state authorities.

"Second, Justice alerted recently-resigned Miami police chief William O'Brien before "Operation Reunion" and reportedly ordered him not to inform Mayor Joe Carollo. The vocally anti-Castro mayor had grown close to the Gonzalez family and might have publicized this news. Still, federal officials should not have meddled with a local government by constructing a wall of silence between a police chief and his popularly elected boss.

"The Department of Justice's contempt for the 11th Circuit Court of Appeals insults the separation of powers. DOJ was not deterred by the court's refusal to grant an order to transfer Elian from his great-uncle to his father. When a three-judge federal panel rejected her plan, Jackboot Janet executed it anyway. Of course, all this could have been avoided had Reno simply waited until May 11 to make her pro-family-reunification case before a judge.

"Bill Clinton and Janet Reno harbor neither respect nor reverence for the Bill of Rights and the Constitution."…"

"This matters gravely, because if the president and attorney general skate past this abuse of power, the next time federal agents storm a private home, waving a flimsy search warrant and beating journalists along the way, the door they batter down won't be Lazaro Gonzalez's. It might be yours."

I want to thank Deroy for allowing me to quote his article so extensively and I want to mention that I could not have described the action and probable consequences of "Operation Reunion" any better.

But, there is more to this sad and tragic story.

First, the fairly short stay of Elian and Juan Miguel at Andrews Air Force Base, near Washington, D.C. While there, the Gonzalez family had a few days of 'family' readjustment, sprinkled with visits from members of the Cuban Interests Section.

Second, the Gonzalez family's relocation from the Air Force Base to the peaceful and luxurious Wye Plantation, in the bordering State of Maryland. But, once in that serene and undisturbed ambiance, the 'support group' sent to the Plantation by Fidel Castro constantly surrounded Elian and his father.

Yes, that's right! Castro had first requested, then demanded and finally received the approval from the Clinton Administration to allow the 'support group" to go to the Plantation to help Elian re-acclimate with his father!

What was the real reason for that "support group" to hover constantly over Elian and his father?

Do you remember that just a few days earlier, on April 13, 2000, Attorney General Reno wrote in her Statement 00-203:

> "…It would be best if the reunification took place at a neutral location—away from the protesters and cameras. That is why we have secured a neutral retreat site near Washington, D.C. where the family can meet away from the glare of the media, the public and Cuban government officials."

I wonder if anyone at the Department of Justice or INS ever questioned themselves about what was the reason for Castro wanting this large "support group" to be so directly involved in the reunification of father and son?

The Cuban government wanted them there! They might not have been Cuban government officials, but certainly they were acting on their behalf!

One more time, "No Cuban government officials were present." Right...!

And, the American authorities wanted to keep Juan Miguel Gonzalez and his reunified family away from the glare of the media, the public and Cuban government officials? Right...!

Did anyone in the Clinton Administration ever think that the so-called "support group" was there to reprogram Elian's mind?

Why was it necessary for Elian's "pediatrician" to be a part of the support group? To my knowledge, Elian was not reported to be sick or injured. Attorney General Reno had stated in her statement of April 22, 2000, "He was examined by a doctor to make sure there were no injuries," before he boarded the U.S. Marshals' aircraft that took him to be reunified with his father.

Was the Cuban communist "pediatrician" allowed to bring her own medications or prescription drugs? Did our authorities check the pediatrician's bags, or were they protected by diplomatic immunity?

Could it be that the "support group" was there to make sure Elian would forget the type of life he had experienced in Miami while under the custody of his great-uncle Lazaro?

Was it perhaps to get Elian prepared to go back to the regime of which his father was apparently a part of in one way or another?

Was it to eliminate his newly acquired idea of liberty and abundance and reconnect him again with the communist atmosphere he would be facing upon returning to his own native country?

For whatever reason, most probably it was Gregory Craig's staff that handled the paper work and requested the necessary visas for the "support group." Without much delay the whole team of "supporters" came to Wye Plantation with the approval and blessing of the Clinton Administration!

15

FATHER AND SON LEAVE THE U.S.

Early this morning I walked to my front yard and hoisted my Flag to the top of the pole as I do every morning. I properly saluted Old Glory and I took a deep breath. Yes, still the same free air I have been breathing ever since I arrived to the United States.

Checking my office calendar as I write this, I noticed that very soon it would be the second anniversary of the 'raid in Miami.' I am sorry to admit that the memories of that day bounced right up into my mind without warning.

Before I proceed in relating the next episode, I will reprint highlights, or better, described as 'punch line' excerpts from most of the statements released by the Department of Justice and the Immigration and Naturalization Service regarding the Elian case:

January 05—"This little boy, who has been through so much, belongs with his father."

January 19—"It is important for the well-being of Elian Gonzalez that the status of this 6-year-old boy be resolved as quickly as possible."

March 28—"…measures to ensure that Elian's transfer occur in a manner that is sensitive to his needs."

April 03— "…it is our hope to begin a smooth and orderly process that will create as little disruption as possible for Elian. We wish to add no further trauma to that which this innocent child has already endured."

April 04—"The focus of the government continues to be on how best to accomplish the reunification of Elian with his father, Juan Miguel Gonzalez."

April 06—"…a cooperative arrangement to reunite Elian in a manner that was least disruptive to everyone involved."

April 06—"…in a manner that is most sensitive to Elian's well-being."

April 07— "Monday's consultation will assist us, not to determining whether the transfer should occur, but how it will occur to cause the least disruption possible."

April 10—"…the doctors will soon be consulting with the INS on the most appropriate way to proceed with Elian's reunion with his father."

April 11—"…to seek an outcome that allows Elian to be reunited with his father in the best way possible—for him, for his family and for the Miami community as a whole."

April 13—"I am prepared to enforce the law. But I want to be clear that if we are compelled to enforce our order, we intend to do so in a reasonable measure way—the approach that we have always taken in this matter. We have the authority to take action, but responsible authority means not only being able to take action—but knowing when and how to take that action…"

"…It represents America and the people who had come to this land of freedom, for opportunity, for the right to speak their mind free of violence."

April 13—"…how to best reunite Elian with his father in the least disruptive manner possible."

April 13—"…A little boy that defines the strength and courage of the human spirit. In the coming days, I urge everyone concerned to think of Elian and to respect the rule of law. Let us make this community a model for what Castro's Cuba is not. Let us make this community a community where people can speak freely without violence and with respect for each other. Let us not disappoint Elian. Let us come together and let us work a way that will best protect the rule of law and this little boy."

April 22—"…unfortunately, the Miami relatives rejected our efforts—leaving us no other option but the enforcement action."
"…It is time to heal the wounds that have divided this community that is so dear to me."

You can read the complete statements for these dates in the final section of this book. And you can also pull the Statements up through the Internet by going to the website WWW.USDOJ.GOV

After reading the above excerpts, do you think any of them reflect what actually happened on April 22, 2000?

Do you remember Elian's face when staring at the muzzle of the rifle aimed in his direction? Was that the Attorney General's concept of "the least disruptive way possible" or "the most appropriate way to proceed with Elian's reunion with his father?"

Do you remember Elian crying hysterically in the arms of the female INS agent when he was rushed out of his great-uncle's home? Was that the Attorney General's idea of how "to ensure that Elian's transfer occur in a manner that was sensitive to his needs?"

If "Operation Reunion" was the "reasonable measure way" that Attorney General Reno had in mind to reunite Elian with his father Juan Miguel, I don't want to think about what she might consider a more drastic measure had she felt the need to approve a more than "reasonable" operation to initiate the reunification of father and son!

I remember Elian's photograph on his way to the emergency room of Hollywood Memorial Hospital on November 25, 1999! While he was strapped to the stretcher he looked scared, but he was not crying or hysterical…

And the Department of Justice "wished to add no further trauma to that which this innocent child has already endured?"

Do you have any doubt as to why it was said a long, long time ago, that some people speak with 'fork tongue'?

Now I certainly can expand that expression, because I feel that some people can also write with 'fork pen,' can type on a 'fork typewriter' or use a 'fork keyboard!'

The same afternoon of the raid, the Miami Gonzalez family flew from Miami to Washington, D.C. and landed at Ronald Reagan National Airport. They wanted to see Elian. Obviously they were very concerned over the welfare and physical condition of the boy after his forceful removal from their home.

They met at our nation's capital with New Hampshire's Senator Robert C. Smith who offered to escort them to try and visit with Elian at Andrews Air Force Base where he was brought in by the U.S. Marshal's aircraft.

Television stations broadcasted the van carrying the Senator and the Cuban family when it was stopped at the Base's gate. The television crews were not allowed close to the entrance and the conversation with the guards could not be heard, but by the following action it was clear that the Senator from the State of New Hampshire was denied access to a United States Air Force Base. Neither Mr. Smith nor the Miami

Gonzalez family was allowed to get through to see the other Gonzalez family from Cuba.

It was no surprise to me that the Miami family was denied access. Juan Miguel was holding the deck of cards and calling the shots.

Most likely he was following the same instructions as his own mother and ex-mother-in-law had earlier received, 'Juan Miguel, you are not allowed to have any family reunions or meetings with your uncles or your cousin. You will not accept any telephone calls from them. You will tell the press you want your son back immediately.'

Of course, I do not have any proof that this type of conversation ever occurred or that this line of instruction was given. But knowing the situation at hand, I can easily picture the list of no's Juan Miguel received before boarding the plane that took him to Washington, D.C.

The last order could have been something like this: 'You'll always have an interpreter to help you with the English problem and when or if you have any doubt about anything, shut up and let your American attorney handle the situation. He will know what to say or do.'

It was really astonishing to me that while Senator Smith was denied access to the American military base, the diplomats from the Cuban Interests Section in Washington, D.C. had an approved 'pass' to get in, and visit Juan Miguel and Elian while they stayed at one of the base's guesthouse! One more time, "No Cuban government officials were present." Right!

MiamiHerald.com published a very interesting column by Ana Radelat. I quote from one paragraph that reads:

> "Luis Fernandez, spokesman for the Cuban Interests Section, said diplomats from the mission have visited Elian and his family at Andrews to bring them mango juice and clothes. "Elian loves mango juice," he said."

I am sure Ms. Radelat double-checked her own notes before publishing her article. I can't help but repeat this one line of her quote: "Elian loves mango juice."

Suddenly Cuban diplomats were wearing the hats of grocery delivery boys, but again, "No Cuban government officials were present." Right!

I want to quote another paragraph from the same article written by Ms. Radelat:

> "Fernandez also said he didn't know if any U.S.-based Cuban diplomats will be able to stay with the family if they move to Wye Plantation on Maryland's rural Eastern Shore, but he said he felt fairly sure they will continue to have access to the boy. "We need access in case we need to supply food or medicine." Fernandez explained."

On April 25, 2000, Juan Miguel Gonzalez, his wife and children were transported to the Wye Plantation for a peaceful reaffirmation of their family ties.

The Plantation compound is located far over the 25 mile limit for the diplomats of the Cuban Interests Section, but the lack of "diplomatic support" toward the family reunification plan was quickly replaced by the "support group" entourage requested by Castro.

April 27, 2000 was a day of partial victories and partial defeats for Lazaro and Juan Miguel.

The 11th Circuit Court of Appeals denied the motion requested by Lazaro that a guardian be named to represent Elian in the Court, but approved the order that the boy should not go any place in the United States that enjoys diplomatic immunity.

On the same day, Juan Miguel's petition to replace Lazaro in the court proceedings was denied, but he was granted the motion to intervene in the case.

It is very interesting that the father would be allowed to intervene in the case of the petition for political asylum filed on behalf of his son, action that he vehemently refused to accept. But he cannot replace his uncle in the court proceedings.

I am glad I am not an attorney. The law is sometimes too confusing for me, but I have no doubt that the Circuit Judges of the U.S. 11th Court of Appeals knew what they were doing.

Finally, Juan Miguel and Gregory Craig were engaged in the legal aspect of Elian's petition for political asylum!

Evidently someone from the Cuban Interests Section complained about the lack of access to Juan Miguel and Elian while at the Wye Plantation and they wanted them back in Washington, D.C. The Cuban diplomats probably felt safe enough to have the Gonzalez family back within their reach after a month of readjustment at the Wye Plantation. The Cuban exile community, it appeared, had accepted the fact that 'Elian belongs with his father' and they could do nothing else but keep praying and watching the legal battle in the Atlanta 'ring.'

Surfing through the Internet I found an article published by Granma International.com, dated May 26, 2000. Granma International is the information branch of the Cuban communist government used to reach the world, reporting their own version about what is happening on the island under their control.

The Cuban communists shot another salvo against the United States as they accused the American authorities of not playing fair in the Elian case! Do you still remember the FOURTH scenario?

Granma International published the following article:

> "May 26, 2000
> "THE REASONS AND NECESSITY FOR JUAN MIGUEL'S MOVE TO WASHINGTON
> "The move of Juan Miguel and his family from the distant Wye Plantation to the city of Washington signifies his first liberation and a second for Elian. That isolated farm with its wide-open spaces was ideal for the first few weeks and allowed Elian to adapt once more to a normal life with his father, his new loving mother and his baby brother, Hianny. He also had the company of his cousin Yasmani, four young school friends and four of their parents, his primary school and his doctor. The time spent there was very worthwhile.

"That small group played a vital role in the extraordinarily rapid adaptation and recovery of the child. Everyone was astonished by his happy face, his smiles and the way he quickly caught up on the five months of schoolwork he missed. The owner, a noble and generous lady of U.S. citizenship, allowed the use of the plantation free of charge. The State Department, the Immigration and Naturalization Service (INS) and Gregory Craig, were all happy with the location, although for differing reasons. However, it had one major disadvantage: its position, some 70 miles from Washington, vas very isolated and was far outside the range of the diplomatic staff of the Cuban Interests Section base in the U.S. capital who are not permitted to travel more than 25 miles from their office. Nonetheless, that wasn't a major worry for them and everything appeared to be harmoniously arranged and organized.

"Problems and obstacles very soon began to appear however. The State Department very abruptly halted Cuban diplomats permission to travel. These were the people responsible for arranging all of the logistics, including the supply of provisions, a mail service and various other indispensable necessities. They also facilitated communication with his family in Cuba in addition to the one or two telephones available at the plantation.

"But it wasn't only that. The U.S. visas of Elian's school friends and their parents were only made valid for 15 days. His doctor had her visa reduced from two months to two weeks. Elian's grandparents, who haven't seen him for six months, were denied any type of visa to visit him. When the doctor passed through Texas on her way back to Cuba, she was told 10 minutes before her plane was due to leave that her visa could now be extended for a few days more.

"It was very worrying that, in response to mafia demands, the INS appointed a psychologist with the right to make systematic inspections. Thus far, this psychologist has had a good attitude, but it signifies a humiliating intrusion into the bosom of the family. The additional imposition of a social worker was inexplicable and her objectives are still unclear. On her second visit she spent her time talking about visits to beaches and similar themes if his stay becomes prolonged. Juan Miguel, who is still understandable sensitive about anything that resembles seduction of his son, took exception to this.

"The reality is that if Juan Miguel remained isolated and without contact with anyone friendly, without the possibility of speaking to the press and without the possibility of making public statements about whatever mischievous untruth is currently circulating, it would be very advantageous for those that are trying to avoid the fundamental need to quickly find a transparent and just solution to this shameful problem that they have arbitrarily and illegally created.

"The lack of medical personnel and other indispensable people, including other children, to support Elian and his family must also be mentioned. These people have been refused U.S. visas. Whilst in that remote country location, seven children, the family and other Cubans were left without access to single doctor.

"In Washington, should it be necessary, they will be able to receive medical attention in a matter of minutes by professional friends in whom they can have confidence.

"It wasn't easy to obtain a suitable house in the capital and various properties were considered. None could be finalized because the State Department blocked each move.

"Finally, the house which will now be used was obtained. This meets a number of requirements, including offering sufficient facilities to allow Elian's schooling to continue.

"Another U.S. citizen has generously donated use of the house free of charge.

"Various noble and friendly people in both Washington and New York who knew of the difficulties, very quickly offered free use of their houses. Included amongst these was the extraordinarily humane religious leader, Joan Brown Campbell.

"At Wye Plantation, the local police were extremely friendly with all the Cubans that were staying there. The control, naturally, was total and absolute. Without doubt, Wye Plantation wasn't the place to await the judgement from Atlanta, a court that in essence was imposed since according to national and international laws it has no jurisdiction over the case.

"The move of Juan Miguel, his family and the other Cubans to Washington constitutes an important event and a new step towards freedom. All that's needed now is the definitive freedom: the rapid return of all of them to Cuba."

Did the Department of Justice, the Immigration and Naturalization Service or anyone within the Clinton Administration read the article published by Granma International? It was written in English, Spanish and probably translated into several other languages, for the whole world to read.

Do you still harbor any doubt about the FOURTH scenario?

On June 1, 2000 Circuit Judges Edmondson, Dubina and Wilson from the United States Court of Appeals for the Eleventh Circuit ruled that the decision of U.S. District Judge K. Michael Moore was correct when he resolved that the determination of the INS was correct in declining to process Elian's application for asylum.

"The judgment of the district court is AFFIRMED" was the very last sentence of the last paragraph of the long document describing the findings and conclusions of the three Circuit Judges. Basically Lazaro Gonzalez's legal battle in the United States courts was finished.

Legally he could and did proceed with more appeals, but his chances to succeed were close to none.

The Department of Justice forthwith issued the following Statement:

"FOR IMMEDIATE RELEASE
"AG
"THURSDAY, JUNE 1, 2000
"(202) 514-2007
"**WWW.USDOJ.GOV**"
"TDD" (202) 514-1888
"STATEMENT BY ATTORNEY GENERAL JANET RENO ON THE 11TH CIRCUIT COURT'S DECISION IN THE ELIAN GONZALEZ CASE.
"We are pleased that the Court has upheld our decision that only Juan Miguel Gonzalez can speak for his son Elian on federal immigration matters. These three federal appellate judges have now

joined with a federal district court judge and a Florida state court judge in recognizing the authority of the INS to make this determination.

"This is an important step in achieving the goal we have sought from the very beginning—to give Juan Miguel and his family the opportunity to return to a life together. I am hopeful that this matter will soon reach a final resolution so that Elian, his father and his family, may resume their lives away from the scrutiny of the media and the uncertainty that the legal battle has caused for them.

"I hope that all of us—regardless of our disagreements about this case—can join together and wish this family well.

"Elian remains in his father's care, but he and his family will not immediately depart the United States. The injunction put in place by the 11th Circuit will remain in effect until the Court's mandate in this case is issued. The INS departure control order put in place on April 22 will remain in place until the injunction is no longer in effect.

"Finally, I want to take a moment to commend the dedicated and absolutely splendid attorneys and staff at the Department of Justice and the Immigration and Naturalization Service who have worked so hard over the past six months on this litigation. They, like so many Americans, were moved by this human drama, and they have devoted long hours to bring about an outcome consistent with the law and our tradition of respect for the parent-child relationship."
00-312

Lazaro's lawyers immediately filed an appeal for the full panel of judges of the U.S. 11th Circuit to review the decision of three of their own judges.

The final curtain for this drama was coming very fast. On June 23rd the U.S. Court of Appeals for the Eleventh Circuit ruled:

"The petition for rehearing is DENIED; and no member of this panel nor other Judge in regular active service on the Court having requested that the Court be polled on rehearing en banc, the Petition for Rehearing En Banc is DENIED."
"..."All injunctions in this case will dissolve on Wednesday, 28

June 2000, at 4:00 in the afternoon (Atlanta time). All further requests for stays or for injunctive relief should be directed to the Supreme Court of the United States."

The Department of Justice immediately acknowledged that decision issuing the following Statement:

"FOR IMMEDIATE RELEASE
"AG
"FRIDAY, JUNE 23, 2000
"(202)-2777
"**WWW.USDOJ.GOV**
"TDD (202) 514-1888
"STATEMENT BY ATTORNEY GENERAL JANET RENO ON THE 11TH CIRCUIT'S DENIAL OF REHEARING IN THE ELIAN GONZALEZ CASE

"WASHINGTON, DC—The 11th Circuit of Appeals today denied the motion by the Miami relatives of Elian Gonzalez for a rehearing or a rehearing en banc in the case of Elian Gonzalez. Attorney General Janet Reno issued the following statement:

"We are pleased that the 11th Circuit Court of Appeals has acted unanimously in denying the motion for rehearing in the case of Elian Gonzalez. Now that the Court has conclusively upheld our decision, I am hopeful that this father and son will soon be able to move on with their lives together."
00-360

The final curtain of the true-life soap opera drama of the boat-wrecked boy came exactly 185 days after his sensational arrival in Hollywood, Florida. On June 28, 2000 the United States Supreme Court refused to hear the appeal of Lazaro Gonzalez to secure asylum for his great-nephew Elian Gonzalez.

The Department of Justice issued their final Statement in the Elian Gonzalez case,

"FOR IMMEDIATE RELEASE

"AG

"WEDNESDAY, JUNE 28, 2000

"(202) 616-2777

"**WWW.USDOJ.GOV**

"TDD (202) 514-1888

"STATEMENT BY ATTORNEY GENERAL JANET RENO ON THE DECISION OF THE SUPREME COURT TO DENY CERTIORRI IN THE CASE OF ELIAN GONZALEZ.

"WASHINGTON, DC—The United States Supreme Court today declined to accept for review the case of Elian Gonzalez. The Court's action means that the injunction put in place by the 11th Circuit Court of Appeals will expire at 4:00 PM eastern time today, and Elian Gonzalez will be permitted to depart the U.S. Attorney General Janet Reno issued the following statement:

"I am very pleased that the Supreme Court has declined to review the case of Elian Gonzalez. The law has provided a process, and this little boy now knows that he can remain with his father. All involved have had an opportunity to make their case—all the way to the highest court in the land. I hope that everyone will accept the Supreme Court's decision and join me in wishing this family and this special little boy, well."

00-373

I doubt there was one single person who had wanted to keep Elian Gonzalez in the land of the free that didn't wish him well. I am sure that many of them had tears in their eyes while watching the departure of the silver aircraft that was taking Elian back to Cuba.

I do not doubt that some day, in the future, the news media will interrupt their programming with the BREAKING NEWS that Elian is back in the hands of the Immigration and Naturalization Service after he successfully beached his own boat or raft on one of the Florida Keys.

At that time he will be old enough to ask for his own political asylum! Who knows? Maybe Juan Miguel, Nersy and Hianny will come along with him, as his passengers!

16

CONCLUSION

I am very pleased you have read this far, and I hope you have had an opportunity to gather your thoughts regarding this case. I am sure you have arrived at your own conclusion after reading all previous fifteen chapters. Do you have the same opinion about this affair as you did before you read this book?

Along these pages I have explained situations and analyzed circumstances of this drama as it was presented to the public. I kept asking questions throughout and I hope I was clear in my presentations of the incidents in order for you to pick up on the main points and the reasons for my inquiries. The answers to some of those questions could have tremendous repercussions in our lives, if not addressed in a firm and concise way.

In these chapters I have cited excerpts, copied statements and asked numerous questions about the Elian case. Would you like to ask me why I wanted to write a book about an event that should be considered long gone—in the past—and irrelevant to the future of our country? You deserve my most candid answer in this regard.

The action that took place in the early morning hours of April 22, 2000 made me write this book!

Why? Because it brought back memories to me of Havana, where the sanctity of our homes were constantly violated by the dictator in control of Cuba's destiny. I honestly wish I had never been a witness to the break in and seizure of Elian right here in the United States of America! I was quite disturbed as I am sure many of you were upon learning of this event.

I came to the U.S. in 1962 yearning to get back the freedom and justice I had lost in the country of my birth. I fondly remember several years later, when raising my right hand in front of a federal judge I promised to respect, uphold and defend the Constitution of the United States of America, against foreign and domestic enemies.

I am a naturalized American citizen and this is my country now. Here is where my wife and children were born and I will honor that promise until the day I die!

I have goose bumps every time I recite, "I pledge allegiance to the Flag of the United States of America and to the Republic for which it stands, one Nation under God, indivisible, with liberty and justice for all."

In those lines I find the most noble thoughts and desires I could aspire to have fulfilled in my lifetime. It summarizes what our country is all about. How many times do I stop to think about what these words mean? Very often, and I fully cherish their every meaning.

Please, bear with me because I have a few more questions...

Was the justice or the liberty of the Gonzalez family usurped from them when their home was overpowered by the drastic decision of the Attorney General of the United States? The door of that family was broken through in the early hours of April 22, 2000.

Those armed agents were following the orders of the chief law enforcement agent of the United States. That early morning para-military action was planned and executed, not against some well-known drug dealers, bank robbers, criminals or extremist terrorists. It was ordered against a family that just had a different point of view from Janet Reno and had challenged, in the court of law, her determinations and orders, under the protection of the same 'rule of law' continuously invoked by the Attorney General.

Did Attorney General Reno ever think of the possibility that those armed agents could have accidentally shot un-armed, emotional and excited demonstrators opposed to her decision?

Would you agree that the first decision taken to release Elian from the INS custody in November 26, 1999, and the para-military operation of April 22, 2000 to get him back, were both wrong…that neither one should have ever happen?

Before giving the order to proceed with "Operation Reunion," did Attorney General Reno give any thought to the possibility that she might have given an okay to an operation that could or would have unfathomable consequences in the future of the United States?

It was reported that a very large amount of Cuban-American registered voters changed their political affiliation after the action of April 22, 2000 from the Democratic Party to the Republican Party or became Independents.

Mark Silva, senior political writer for The Miami Herald wrote on April 25, 2000 about the reaction of the Cuban-American voters and I quote from his article:

> "Scores of Cuban-Democrats on Monday (April 24, 2000) registered their protest of the Clinton Administration predawn seizure of Elian Gonzalez by severing ties to the Democratic Party."

In his article Mark Silva quoted Bob Poe, Chairman of the Florida Democratic Party saying:

> "That is going to be part of my agenda this week, to sort of figure out what we need to do there. We want to make sure we are building bridges and not tearing them down."

It certainly was a colossal task Mr. Poe had set upon himself, to organize a 'damage control' campaign to change the thinking of the Cuban-American Democrat voters.

It would be very hard to erase from anybody's mind the photo of the frightened Elian facing a machine gun pointed in his direction when he was in the arms of Donato Dalrymple, while both where trying to hide in a bedroom closet. The image of Elian's contorted and scared face, crying in the arms of the female INS agent when he was carried out from the home of his great-uncle is probably still fresh in the memory of many Cuban-American ex-democrats voters.

Anyway, even my good friend Dr. Watson could have deducted that those switching and breaking their political alliance to the Democratic Party would result in a minus count for the democrat candidate in the oncoming presidential election of November 7, 2000.

Could it be that those scores of Cubans changing party affiliation were the votes that actually determined the final tally of the polls on that election in the State of Florida? Even with every little hanging "chad" and every noticeable "dimple" being deeply scrutinized under magnifying lenses, the final re-count was dramatically close!

I will leave it to the historians and scholars to come up with the answer to that question.

In retrospect, I cannot find any reason in my mind to be critical of Lazaro Gonzalez or his efforts to keep Elian in the United States. He followed and traveled all the legal avenues that our laws offered to him in his desire to fulfill the wish of his great-nephew's mother.

From the beginning of this dramatic affair Lazaro was constantly under the advice of reputable lawyers. Very respected and important American personalities also encouraged him in his endeavors, along with uncountable supporters.

But, 'at the end of every day' he knew that he was fighting the big Goliath of the north with only white sand filling the pouch of his sling.

I am sure he knew that after losing his case in the court of U.S. District Judge Moore he had a hard up-hill fight. His last option could be to appeal all the way to the Supreme Court of the United States. And, he must have had no doubt in his mind that if or when the Supreme Justices declined to hear his plea or rule against his petition, everything was over and he would have to pack Elian's things and let him go back to Cuba!

Therefore, what was the reason for the Justice Department to rush and remove the boy by force? I have tried very hard and many times to find logical or legal justifications for that forceful action, but I could not find any satisfactory answers.

Attorney General Reno must have had some other very important reasons for ordering that attack, because her statement, "They thought they could ignore us" as a reason why she made such an extreme decision is remarkably weak, and in many ways irresponsible.

And, I wonder what was in her mind when she continued with her explanations: "We had tried to be very patient with them to conduct a voluntary transfer, and the time comes when the law must be enforced."

"…Unfortunately the Miami relatives rejected our efforts—leaving us no other option but the enforcement action."

Future generations might consider that statement as a new legal twist: 'You must enforce the rule of law by all means, even if that means taking an action that breaks the rule of law itself.'

Fortunately it's not very often, but sometimes a terrible thought comes to my mind when I think about the raid in Miami. I try to forget about it and erase that thought immediately! It is too awful…too terrifying…to even think about it!

I was just a young child living in Cuba when President Roosevelt told the American people after the attack on Pearl Harbor on December 7, 1941 that they had nothing to fear but fear itself.

Yes I do realize that time will heal my wounds…

The final three questions:

> One—Did the Attorney General of the United States flutter and cave in under pressure by the demands for action by Juan Miguel Gonzalez, who was under the legal advice of Gregory Craig and while "Castro himself was calling the shots" all the way from Cuba?
>
> Two—Was it a SHAME the way Ms. Reno handled this case?
>
> Three—Was it a SHAM cunningly perpetrated by Castro?

I am and will be very respectful of your conclusions and opinion.

I have mine…and they are carved so very deeply into my heart!

COPIES OF CORRESPONDENCE AND E-MAILS

At the very beginning of this book I mentioned that I would not try to force my opinion on you, but you deserve to know how I felt during the developing Elian affair.

Only nine days before the raid in Miami I sent a letter to my Congressman Charles T. Canady. The entire letter is reprinted here:

April 13, 2000
The Honorable Charles T. Canady
United States House of Representatives
12th Congressional District
1222 Longworth House Office Building
Washington, DC 20515

Dear Representative Canady:

We can rest assured that Ms Janet Reno, our Attorney General, is not King Solomon…

During the past four months a sad and unbelievably tragic true-life soap opera has unfolded before the whole world and specifically to the American citizens. The case of Elian Gonzalez has captured the attention of everyone with obvious opposite points of view.

The heart of many cry out loud for the young boat-wrecked child to stay here in the land of the free, which was evidently his mother's desire and intention. She tragically and unfortunately lost her life fleeing the land of communism. Had she been successful in her brave endeavor to reach the land of opportunity, there would have been no consideration in returning Elian to his communist father in Cuba, even if or when he requested so.

The opinion of the majority with legalistic minds is that Elian should be returned to his father Juan Miguel Gonzalez as he requested on November 27, 1999. He wanted his son back arguing that the boy was taken from Cuba without his knowledge or consent. They argue and claim that the surviving parent has the legal and lawful authority over how his offspring should be raised.

I understand that the United States Coast Guard has specific orders to intercept any vessel, boat or raft in the open sea and return the occupants to the original country of departure. The INS would only consider asylum for those persons who succeeded in landing on AMERICAN SOIL.

Let's stop here, momentarily…

By a divine miracle Elian survived two days floating on an inner tube in the deep waters of the Gulfstream and the little boy was rescued way offshore by two fishermen who radioed the U.S. Coast Guard informing them of their discovery. The Coast Guard officers rushed the child to the nearest hospital in Hollywood, Florida for immediate medical attention. This certainly was a very humane and most commendable action by our servicemen.

Then another miracle occurred immediately…In less than two days Elian recovered enough to be released from the hospital in Hollywood where he was receiving medical attention and our authorities found Elian's relatives living in Miami, placing him under their custody and care. His father in Cuba learned 'one way or another' that his ex-wife had perished in her attempt to reach America but his son survived and was paroled by the INS and under the custody of his great-uncle Lazaro Gonzalez.

Today, April 13, 2000 almost four and a half months after the boy's dramatic arrival to the United States, Elian is the center of the most highly politicized tug of war. Our Attorney General is telling us that she is following the law and wants to return Elian to his father so he can take his son to Cuba.

I am fascinated by the arguments and logic used my Ms. Reno. The same laws our officials in Washington are trying to apply now were already in force on November and December of 1999. Besides, what happened to our system granting legal avenues to solve a problem?

As a proud naturalized American I know I will not gain any grace from my old countrymen with the following statement. I certainly believe that while my heart wants to keep Elian here, away from the grip and absolute control of the communist regimen controlling Cuba, my logic tells me that he belongs with his surviving parent, had his father COME IMMEDIATELY to claim his son.

It must be noted that the emotional and vocal Cuban community that opposes Elian's return knows firsthand the hardships involved in living under a totalitarian regime as the one imposed in communist Cuba. Castro has found a way to further irritate the Cubans here by showing his supposed concern for family. Many of them still have relatives in Cuba that have not been able to leave the red paradise because the communist ruling and oppressive policies.

I certainly can't believe that our smart and highly educated officials in Washington did not have any idea that Castro would get so fully involved in this case. He will use every angle he can to appear to be the family-oriented leader he is not. After more than forty-one years it seems that Washington still does not understand the communist Cuban lone ranger, President Castro. Some of his own relatives asked political asylum and ran away from him!

Time heals almost any wound, if treated timely and in the proper manner. I am sure that had this situation been take care of quickly and without hesitation, back on November 27, 1999, no one would be hurting as much as many are now. At the present moment, it requires the wisdom of King Solomon...There does not seem to be any right answer...

I must conclude this lengthy letter by trying to explain the loudly vocal and emotional Cuban feelings on this case and of any other one involving Castro and his regime.

Think of an unlikely and impossible change of our form of government in the United States. Suppose that our democratic system is forcibly replaced by a dictator and his ruling is imposed over everyone here. Shortly after taking over, the new government confiscates all personal land, property and business without proper compensation.

Worse! They tell you were to live, were you can work and how to educate your children. Some of those that refuse to accept the new rules are executed or imprisoned. Others are forced to leave the land of their birth and live in a foreign land.

How do you think the politically exiled American would feel when anything happened in their new country involving anything regarding the dictator that pushed them out from their native land?

The answer to this hypothetical situation will explain the Cuban exile's feeling about Castro, his cohorts and the communist regime they represent and force on their suffered captive island.

I thank you for reading this long letter,

Respectfully yours,

Cesar Guerra

Two days after the 'raid' in Miami, I sent several e-mails to members of the Congress of the United States.

The following e-mail went to the Speaker of the House in Washington D.C.

Subject: A black mark in the USA history book.

Date: 04-24-2000 10:04:22 PM Eastern Daylight time.

Rep. J. Dennis Hastert, Speaker of the House of Representatives: I pray that the respectful members of the Congress of the United States find the truth about this ugly and scary episode of the raid of the Gonzalez family in Miami. In 1962 I fled communist Cuba and came to the land of the free and home of the brave and became a proud naturalized American citizen few years later. The latest action of the Clinton Administration brought back to me memories of Havana, where the government forces has the 'right' to raid and invade the privacy of any citizen. The Gonzalez family in Miami is being accused of breaking the law and holding the child against the order of the Justice Department. Well, I want to know why, if they broke the law, they were not arrested or summoned in due time for such violations. Instead, the 'Justice Department' broke their doors in a 'show of force' that would make communist Cuba green with envy. Justice for whom? Craig and Castro? Isn't this Mr. Craig the same lawyer that represented President Clinton in the White House affair couple years back? Is President Clinton paying back the favor? The order and permission to attack was signed by a magistrate at the last minute, without notification to the Miami family or their lawyer. Don't you think this is a cover-up to a 'successful' action, regardless your point of view in this matter? I am sending a similar e-mail to my representative, Congressman Charles Canady and I hope that the Judiciary Committee of the House of Representatives has a full hearing in this ugly and unlike-American action that one more time is inflaming the passion and emotions of so many while dividing again the citizens of our beloved country. Thank you for your time in reading my comment and I expect to hear of a quick action in this matter.

Sincerely,

Cesar Guerra

E-MAIL TO REPRESENTATIVE CHARLES CANADY:

Subject: Following what law?

Date: 04-24-2000 09:10:05 PM Eastern Daylight Time

Rep. Charles Canady: In 1962 I fled communist Cuba and came to the land of the free and home of the brave. The latest action of the Clinton Administration brought me memories of Havana, were the government forces has the 'right' to raid and invade the privacy of any citizen. The Gonzalez family in Miami is being accused of breaking the law, and holding the child against the order of the Department of Justice. I want to know why if they broke the law they were not arrested and notified in due time of such violation. Instead the "Justice Department" broke doors in a 'show' of force that will make communist Cuba green with envy. It was justice for whom? Craig and Castro? The permission to attack was signed by a magistrate at the last minute, without notification to the Miami family or their lawyer. Don't you think this is another cover-up? Thank you for your time in reading my comments.

Sincerely,

Cesar Guerra

E-MAIL TO SENATOR CONNIE MACK:

Subject: Rule of law?

Date: 04-24-2000 08:44:19 PM Eastern Daylight Time

Senator Connie Mack: In 1962 I came from Cuba to the land of the free and home of the brave. The latest action of the Clinton Administration brought me back to Havana where the government forces has the 'right' to invade the privacy of a citizen. The Gonzalez family in Miami is being accused of breaking the law, and holding the child against the order of the Department of Justice. I want to know why if they broke the law they were not arrested and notified in due time of such violation. Instead the "Justice Department" broke doors in a "show" of force that will make communist Cuba green with envy. Justice for whom? Craig and Castro? Thank you for your time in reading my comments.

Sincerely,

Cesar Guerra

E-MAIL TO SENATOR ROBERT 'BOB' GRAHAM:

Subject: Totalitarian Government Style Attack

Date: 04-24-2000 08:32:46 pm eastern Daylight Time

Senator Bob Graham: With pride and admiration I heard your statement on TV about the promise from President Clinton to you that a raid on the Miami family's home, in the dead of the night, would not happen. I just finished watching the program Crossfire (CNN) and the White House states that President Clinton denies ever having such a conversation with you. Even though I am registered Republican, I respect you as my Senator & truly believe that you are a man of integrity and moral principals. Please tell me that you stand by your statement. Thank you.

Sincerely,

Cesar Guerra

STATEMENTS FROM INS AND DOJ

The following transcripts are copy of press releases and statements published by the Department of Justice in the website: **www.ins.usdoj. gov/graphics/publicaffairs/statements/Elian.htm**.

All these documents carry the printed seal of the Department of Justice on the top left corner.

STATEMENT
January 5, 2000
INS DECISION IN THE ELIAN GONZALEZ CASE
Doris Meissner
Commissioner
Immigration and Naturalization Service
The case of Elian Gonzalez has been a difficult one for several reasons. Elian Gonzalez is a six-year-old boy, too young to make legal decisions for himself. In this circumstance, the U.S. Immigration and Naturalization Service (INS) had to decide who could legally speak for him on immigration issues. This task was complicated by the fact that several people other than Elian's father—Great uncle as well as three lawyers—claimed to represent him. As a result, INS met with the father in Cuba, and separately, with the great uncle and the lawyers in Miami. After careful evaluation of the relevant facts, INS has determined that Mr. Juan Gonzalez of Cuba has the sole legal authority to speak on behalf of his son, Elian, regarding Elian's immigration status in the United States.

There is no question that Mr. Gonzalez is Elian's father. Moreover, Mr. Gonzalez has had a close and continuous parental relationship with his son. During INS' interviews with Elian's father, he provided vivid details about his parental relationship with his son and about the nature of the bond they share as father and son. He provided extensive documentation about Elian's schooling and his medical and health histories, as well as photographs depicting the activities in which he and his other family members frequently participated with Elian. This scope of information and level of detail Mr. Gonzalez provided helped inform INS as to the nature and closeness of the relationship Mr. Gonzalez shared with his son Elian. INS has not uncovered any information that might call into question Mr. Gonzalez's parental and legal rights with regard to Elian's immigration status.

During INS' two meetings with Mr. Gonzalez, his wishes for Elian were discussed at some length. He made it very clear during both of those meetings that he wants Elian returned to him as soon as possible. Based on these meetings, INS believes that he is expressing his true wishes, and therefore we have determined that Elian should be reunited with his father, Mr. Gonzalez.

INS has advised both Mr. Gonzalez and Elian's great uncle in Miami of this decision, and is prepared to work with all the parties involved to make the appropriate arrangements for Elian's return to his father by January 14, 2000.

Having reached a decision, INS believes there are several ways this decision can be implemented. The United States has discussed with the Government of Cuba their consideration of allowing Mr. Gonzalez, Elian's father, to travel to the United States to accompany Elian home. INS also has offered Elian's great-uncle in Miami and any member of his Miami family an opportunity to escort Elian back to Cuba. In addition, third parties have offered to assist in facilitating Elian's return to his father. INS is ready to work with the family and others to make appropriate arrangement for Elian to be reunited with his father. We believe this decision can be carried out without INS' taking charge of Elian.

The decision has been based on the facts and the law. Both U.S. and international law recognize the unique relationship between parent and child, and family reunification has long been a cornerstone of both American immigration law and INS practice.

It is our hope that with the knowledge of today's decision, the Miami relatives will agree to cooperate and work together, with either Elian's father or a third party, to facilitate Elian's return to his father. This little boy, who has been through so much, belongs with his father. We urge everyone involved to understand, respect and uphold the bond between parent and child and the laws of the United States.

-INS-

STATEMENT

January 19, 2000

DEPARTMENT OF JUSTICE AND IMMIGRATION AND NAT-URALIZATION SERVICE JOINT STATEMENT OF FEDERAL COURT ACTION REGARDING ELIAN GONZALEZ.

Attorneys in Miami have filed a federal district court action related to the INS decision regarding Elian Gonzalez. The U.S. Department of Justice (DOJ) and the Immigration and Naturalization Service (INS) are fully prepared to quickly respond to this action.

It is important for the well-being of Elian Gonzalez that the status of this 6-year-old boy be resolved as quickly as possible. We will therefore ask the court to expeditiously address this matter. Last week INS decided to extend the January 14 date for the reunification of Elian Gonzalez with his father in order to accommodate federal court action. On January 4, INS determined that Juan Gonzalez, the father of Elian Gonzalez, has the sole legal authority to speak for his son on immigration issues. This decision was based on the facts and the law, and recognizes the bond that exists between parent and child. Last week Attorney General Janet Reno reaffirmed her support for the INS decision.

In keeping with normal DOJ and INS policy, we will not publicly discuss the specifics of issues pending before the courts.

FOR IMMEDIATE RELEASE
AG
JANUARY 22,2000
(202) 616-2777
WWW.USDOJ.GOV
TDD (202) 514-1888
ATTORNEY GENERAL AND COMMISSIONER MEISSNER STATEMENT
Washington, D.C.—Attorney General Janet Reno and I.N.S. Commissioner Doris Meissner met today with Mariela Quintana, Raquel Rodriguez, grandmothers of Elian Gonzalez, and Dr. Joan Brown Campbell, Bob Edgar and Oscar Bolioli, of the National Council of Churches, as well as Oden Marichal of the Cuban Council of Churches.The Attorney General and Commissioner Meissner issued the following statement:

- "Ms. Quintana and Ms. Rodriguez made a very compassionate and heartfelt plea to be reunited with their grandson. They asked when Elian could return to his father and the rest of his family in Cuba. We explained that this matter is now in federal court but that we will seek resolution as expeditiously as possible. We accepted a letter from Ms. Quintana and Ms. Rodriguez which reiterated the issues raised in today's meeting.

- We maintain that the law recognizes the unique relationship between parent and child and that family reunification has long been a cornerstone of both American immigration law and INS practice."

00-040

STATEMENT
February 18, 2000
INS RESPONSE TO MR. JUAN GONZALEZ

The U.S. Immigration and Naturalization Service (INS) today informed Mr. Juan Gonzalez, father of Elian Gonzalez, that the INS remains fully committed to reuniting him with his son Elian as soon as possible, consistent with legal procedures. The INS told Mr. Gonzalez that after careful consideration of his request to move Elian, the agency does not plan to change the temporary care arrangements for Elian at this time.

The decision was made in response to requests from Juan Gonzalez that Elian be moved from the care of Lazaro Gonzalez and placed in the care of Manolo Gonzalez, both of whom are Juan Gonzalez uncles. INS emphasized to Mr. Gonzalez that Elian's current care arrangements are only temporary while a federal court reviews INS' decision. INS stated that the agency shares Mr. Gonzalez' concern that Elian be well cared for, and therefore will request information from Lazaro Gonzalez concerning the credentials of any psychiatrist or psychologist who has seen Elian, as well as an explanation of any treatment that may have been prescribed for him. INS also will request information regarding Elian's schooling.

The INS advised Juan Gonzalez that a Miami-based nongovernmental organization conducted a post-placement visit to verify that Lazaro Gonzalez's home was an adequate setting for Elian's temporary care. INS indicated that transferring Elian temporarily to a new and unfamiliar environment would not be advisable for the child after already experiencing the trauma of leaving his home in Cuba and losing his mother. Instead, INS will continue to focus its efforts on returning Elian to his father.

INS also stated that it is aware of Lazaro Gonzalez' past convictions for driving under the influence of alcohol, but that the information INS has at present does not suggest that Lazaro Gonzalez' home is not an adequate environment for Elian's temporary care at this time. INS is prepared, however, to revisit this issue if additional relevant information becomes available.

Regarding Mr. Gonzalez' concern about the Miami family's request that the federal district court appoint a 'guardian ad litem' for Elian, INS stated that the government is preparing a response to that motion which will be filed with the court within the next few days.

INS reiterated to Mr. Gonzalez that it is committed to resolving this matter as fairly and expeditiously as possible.

STATEMENT
March 28, 2000
ELIAN GONZALEZ

Officials representing the Department of Justice and the Immigration and Naturalization Service met with attorneys representing Lazaro Gonzalez this morning at the INS District Office in Miami. The purpose of the meeting was to discuss the ramifications of parole termination and the orderly return of Elian to his father including, most importantly, measures to ensure that Elian's transfer occur in a manner that is sensitive to his needs.

While INS has always had the authority to implement its decision, we have gone to great lengths to bring about a resolution that is carried out in a manner that creates as little disruption for Elian as possible. Far from depriving Lazaro Gonzalez of his right to appeal, we have attempted to accommodate his interest in obtaining review by the Court of Appeals while assuring a prompt and orderly reunion of Elian and his father if the District Court's decision is affirmed. This assurance is consistent with federal law and normal INS procedures.

Under federal immigration law and INS procedure, the government routinely requests written assurances that individuals paroled into the United States will comply with the terms of their parole. The simple assurance we have sought from Lazaro Gonzalez is that he will cooperate with an orderly transfer of Elian Gonzalez in the event of an adverse ruling by the U.S. Court of Appeals and barring emergency injunctive relief from the Supreme Court. Lazaro Gonzalez will be meeting with INS and Justice Department officials tomorrow afternoon. We hope that, at that time, he will agree to the very reasonable conditions that we have set out as a condition of Elian's continued parole.

From the beginning, we have been mindful of the fact that at the center of this case is a six-year-old boy who has been through a terrible ordeal. We are concerned for him and will continue to try to resolve this matter in a way that avoids additional trauma to him. It has been nearly 12 weeks since the Commissioner's decision, and four months since Elian was separated from his father and lost his mother. As District Court Judge Moore said in his ruling last week, "Each passing day is another day lost between Juan Gonzalez and his son."

We continue to urge everyone involved to work together to understand, respect and uphold the bond between parent and child and the laws of the United States.

STATEMENT
March 29, 2000
DOJ AND INS STATEMENT ON ELIAN GONZALEZ
The Department of Justice (DOJ) and the Immigration and Natural-
ization Service (INS have decided to continue discussions concerning
Elian Gonzalez. The parties will meet at the Office of the U.S. Attor-
ney in Miami at 9:30 a.m. tomorrow. The government will therefore
defer revocation of Elian's parole status for a 24-hour period.

STATEMENT
March 30, 2000
DOJ AND INS STATEMENT ON THE ELIAN GONZALEZ CASE

The Department of Justice (DOJ) and the Immigration and Naturalization Service (INS have agreed to resume discussions with Lazaro Gonzalez and his legal counsel at 10 a.m. on Monday, April 3. In the meantime, Elian's parole status will continue unchanged, and he will be allowed to remain in Lazaro Gonzalez' care. Elian's parole is therefore extended until 9 am, Tuesday, April 4.

All parties are monitoring developments concerning the possible arrival of Juan Miguel Gonzalez in the United States.

The Department of Justice and the INS have approached these discussions in good faith, and we hope to continue to move forward on Monday. We continue to urge the community to recognize the importance of the bond between parent and child as well as the need to uphold the laws of the United States.

—INS—

STATEMENT
April 3, 2000
DISCUSSIONS IN ELIAN GONZALEZ CASE
Discussions will resume at 10:00 a.m. Tuesday, regarding how to begin the transfer of care of Elian Gonzalez to his father, Juan Miguel Gonzalez. No final decision has been reached in this matter, but the discussions are continuing in good faith.

The scheduled revocation of Elian's parole tomorrow has been superseded by the expected arrival of Juan Miguel Gonzalez in the United States. The Miami relatives have long said they wanted the father to come here. The father has indicated that he wants to be here with his son. Once Mr. Gonzalez arrives, the Immigration and Naturalization Service will begin transferring parole care from Lazaro Gonzalez to the boy's father. The transfer of parole custody does not mean that the child will be immediately removed from the home of his great-uncle. Instead, it is our hope to begin a smooth and orderly process that will create as little disruption as possible for Elian. We wish to add no further trauma to that which this innocent child has already endured.

We ask everyone involved who cares about this little boy to work with us to allow these talks to go forward in an orderly and respectful way in an effort to reach a cooperative solution.

STATEMENT
April 4, 2000
STATEMENT ON THE ELIAN GONZALEZ CASE
The attorneys representing Lazaro Gonzalez have asked that we continue our discussions on Thursday, April 6 at 9:30 a.m. We are sensitive to the challenges the family members are facing and have agreed to do so. We will meet again on Thursday to discuss the transfer of Elian to his father.

The focus of the government continues to be on how best to accomplish the reunification of Elian with his father, Juan Miguel Gonzalez.

—INS—

FOR IMMEDIATE RELEASE
DAG
THURSDAY, APRIL 6, 2000
(202) 616-2777
WWW.USDOJ.GOV
TDD (202) 514-1888

STATEMENT OF DEPUTY ATTORNEY GENERAL ERIC HOLDER, JR. ON THE ARRIVAL OF JUAN MIGUEL GONZALEZ

A short time ago, Elian's father, Juan Miguel Gonzalez, arrived here in the United States. He came with his wife and he came with his infant son. Their arrival is a welcome development in a case that has captured everyone's attention ever since young Elian arrived at our shores.

At the core of this case is a little boy—so young that he does not have the capacity to make legal decisions for himself. He has a father who has clearly enjoyed a close and continuous relationship with Elian from the moment he was born. And he also has relatives in Miami who undoubtedly care deeply for this little boy.

There have been some who have claimed that the government has acted in a heavy handed manner. I reject this notion. In January, the INS decided—and we agreed—that only Juan Miguel has the authority to speak on his son's behalf regarding immigration matters. Mr. Gonzalez has clearly and sincerely stated that he wants to be reunited with his son.

In an effort to be fair and most importantly to consider young Elian's well-being, we did not immediately implement our decision—even though we had the authority to do so. Instead, we urged the Miami relatives to work out a cooperative arrangement to reunite Elian in a manner that was least disruptive to everyone involved.

Since then, a federal court has upheld our decision. Then, demonstrating further restraint, we offered the Miami relatives an opportunity to appeal the court's ruling so long as they did not assure further open-ended delays.

Today we are as committed as ever to reuniting the two in a manner that is most sensitive to Elian's well-being.

This morning we will continue discussing these issues with the lawyers for the relatives in Miami, we strongly believe that Juan Miguel Gonzalez's presence here will move the process forward and will allow the parties to quickly effectuate a transfer of Elian to his father.

I have a six-year-old daughter. And as a father, I cannot imagine the anguish of being separated from my daughter due to circumstances beyond my control. That is one reason that I believe reuniting Elian with his father is not only a matter of federal law, it is not a matter of immigration law, it is simply the right thing to do.

This father and his son need to be together. And in the coming days we will do all that we can to ensure that happens.

00-178

STATEMENT

April 6, 2000

STATEMENT OF THE DEPARTMENT OF JUSTICE AND
IMMIGRATION AND NATURALIZATION SERVICE

We are very disappointed that, after several days of meetings, the
Miami relatives of Elian Gonzalez continue to refuse to return Elian to
his father, Juan Miguel Gonzalez.

Officials from the Department of Justice and the Immigration and
Naturalization Service had extended their discussions with the relative's attorneys and deferred revocation of Elian's parole status for a
week in an effort to reach a cooperative solution.

Recognizing how much Lazaro Gonzalez and his family care for this
child, we had hoped that the relatives would understand the importance of reuniting Elian and his father, with as little continued disruption.

Unfortunately, the extended discussions did not result in assurances
from the relatives that they would voluntarily transfer custody of Elian.
These standard assurances are required by federal law as a condition of
parole. Instead, the attorneys continued to revisit the issue of whether
Elian should be reunited with his father, as opposed to discussing how
best to reunite them.

In January, the INS ruled, and the Attorney General affirmed, that the
father speaks for the son. For the past four months, Juan Miguel
Gonzalez has made it very clear that he wants to be reunited with his
six-year-old son. Last month, a federal court sustained the decision of
the Commissioner of the INS and the Attorney General. At any point
along the way, the INS and the Department of Justice could have
implemented the ruling immediately, but instead we went to extraordinary lengths to try to resolve this matter in a cooperative manner.

We will soon provide the relatives in Miami with a letter setting forth
the process for reuniting Elian with his father, who arrived in the
United States earlier this morning. We still hope for an orderly process
for reuniting Elian with his father.

FOR IMMEDIATE RELEASE
AG
APRIL 7, 2000
(202) 616-2777
WWW.USDOJ.GOV
TDD (202) 514-1888
STATEMENT OF ATTORNEY GENERAL RENO

Today, I met with Elian's father, Juan Miguel Gonzalez—a man who expressed in a very clear and a very heartfelt manner his sincere desire to have his son returned to him as soon as possible. He obviously loves Elian very much. All you had to do is look at him, and see him, to see how much he loves this little boy.

The meeting was only with a very small group of people. Mr. Gonzalez was joined by his wife and their 6-month-old baby boy and his lawyer, Gregory Craig. I was joined by INS Commissioner Doris Meissner, Deputy Attorney General Eric Holder, a member of his staff, and an official U.S. government translator. No Cuban officials were present.

During the hour-long meeting, Mr. Gonzalez and I had a very open and honest discussion. Throughout, he repeated what he had said time and time again—he wants his son back.

Four months ago, Elian Gonzalez came to our shores after his mother perished at sea. While his immigration status was being resolved, he was placed in the temporary care of his great uncle who lives in Miami. As with any similar arrangement, Elian's temporary custody was conditioned on the understanding that the care-providers will abide by the instructions of the Immigration and Naturalization Service.

In December, INS officials—on two separate occasions—interviewed Mr. Gonzalez in Cuba. Again, no Cuban officials were present. Both times, Mr. Gonzalez asserted his plea to have his child returned to him—and he said he had no desire to live in the United States.

I wholeheartedly reject Cuba's system of government. Mr. Gonzalez and I do not share the same political beliefs.

But it is not our place to punish a father for his political beliefs or for where he wants to raise his child. Indeed, it we were to start judging parents on the basis of their political beliefs, we would change the concept of family for the rest of time.

After meeting with Mr. Gonzalez in Cuba, INS officials also met with relatives in Miami. We wanted to give the relatives an opportunity to provide any information they could that could be relevant to the decision.

In January, after the interviews, the INS Commissioner announced her decision that, not only did the father speak for the son, but that the father's wishes were indeed to have his son with him.

From that moment, nothing prevented the United States government from immediately taking action to reunite the father and son. There was no court order. No stay. No injunction. But instead of moving hastily, we gave the relatives in Miami a chance to challenge our decision in federal court. A federal court sustained our judgement, stating 'each passing day is another day lost between Juan Gonzalez and his son.

Thereafter, we again remained willing to postpone the reunion because we wanted to give the relatives every chance to argue their case in the federal appellate court. All we asked for in return was a pledge that—at the end of the day—when the appeals process had run its course, the Miami relatives would turn over Elian to his father voluntarily. They were unwilling to provide us with that assurance.

For the past several weeks we have engaged in discussions with the relatives to try to come to a cooperative arrangement for reuniting Elian with his father. But instead of discussing how Elian should be reunited, the attorneys for the relatives continued to demand that we re-visit the issue of whether Elian should be reunited. That is not what the law provides.

It has been nearly twelve weeks since the Commissioner's decision, and four months since Elian was found at sea. It is time for this little boy, who has been through so much, to be with his father. The relatives say it would be wrenching to take him from the home. Four months is no substitute for six years for a father who has had such an important role in raising such a wonderful boy.

The law is very clear. Clearly, a child who has lost his mother belongs with his sole surviving parent, especially one with who the child has shared such a close and continuous relationship with his son.

I understand and respect with all my heart the deep-seated beliefs which the Cuban exile community feels on this subject. Cuba is a repressive society. A society ruled by a dictator from whom thousands have fled. Over the past four decades, Cubans have come to the United States to seek freedom and to seek a better way of life. As a result, Miami has prospered and grown. It is a wonderful city, which I love very, very much.

I know most people within the Cuban community [who] differ with my decision [...] have the best interest of Elian at heart. Many of them risked their lives to come to his country. They want him to have the opportunity that they have had. But in the end I believe that they also understand that this is a nation of laws by which all must abide. And it is a nation whose law and foundation recognize that there is a bond, a special, wonderful, sacred bond between a father and a son-one that I intend to uphold.

Yesterday, Mr. Gonzalez came to our country to be reunited with his son. Today, we move forward with that reunification.

Early next week, we will give instructions to the relatives on when and where Elian is to be turned over to his father. And at that time, the INS will formally transfer parole care to the father.

By letter today we are asking the relatives to meet on Monday with two eminent psychiatrists and a distinguished psychologist to determine how the transfer can take place with as little disruption for Elian as possible. The three experts have informed us that the best way to proceed is to effect the reunification promptly. Monday's consultation will assist us, not in determining whether the transfer should occur, but how it will occur to cause the least disruption possible.

I have been in California, in Chicago, in Chile, in Costa Rica, in these past four months. I have been in my own hometown and I have been in Washington. This case has struck the heart and soul of the world.

I urge everybody involved to move forward to effect this reconciliation and reunification as soon as possible. Elian deserves the very, very best and the best we can give him for he has been through so much. In his own way, rather than tear us apart, he has brought us together to understand the strength of the human spirit. Let us not disappoint him.

00-189

STATEMENT
April 10, 2000
DOJ/INS STATEMENT ON THE ELIAN GONZALEZ CASE

The meeting between Elian's Miami relatives and the three experts in child psychiatry and psychology has concluded. Based on the doctors' meeting yesterday with Elian's father, Juan Miguel Gonzalez, and their meeting today with Elian's Miami relatives, the doctors will soon be consulting with the Immigration and Naturalization Service (INS) on the most appropriate way to proceed with Elian's reunion with his father.

These consultations will serve to inform INS' decision on the best way to proceed in reuniting Elian with his father in a way that's the least disruptive to Elian. Subsequently, INS will give instructions to the Miami family on how this transfer will occur. We continue to believe that

Elian's well being is best served if the Miami relatives participate in an active and responsible way in preparing Elian prior to the transfer, as well as in supporting him during and after he is reunited with his father.

Elian and his father, Juan Miguel, have been separated for more than four months. We hope that Elian's Miami relatives and everyone involved with this little boy will be supportive of him and his father during this time.

—INS—

FOR IMMEDIATE RELEASE
AG
Tuesday, April 11, 2000
(202) 616-2777
WWW.USDOJ.GOV
TDD (202) 514-1888
STATEMENT BY ATTORNEY GENERAL JANET RENO FOL-
LOWING MEETING WITH MAYORS OF MIAMI
Attorney General Janet Reno and INS Commissioner Doris Meissner
met today with Miami-Dade County Mayor Alex Penelas and Miami
City Mayor Joe Carollo. The Attorney General issued the following
statement:

- "The meeting with Mayors Penelas and Carollo was productive and I welcomed their suggestions on how we can best achieve an orderly reunification of Elian with his father.

- "We all agreed that helping to bring the family together to work out this orderly transition would be desirable, but I also stressed that the transfer of Elian to the care of his father must move forward without delay.

- "We agreed to continue working together to seek an outcome that allows Elian to be reunited with his father in the best way possi- ble—for him, for his family, and for the Miami community as a whole."

00-198

LETTER SENT TO LAZARO GONZALEZ

April 12, 2000

Dear Mr. Gonzalez:

The goal of the Department of Justice and the Immigration and Naturalization Service is to ensure that Elian's transition to his father's care is as peaceful as possible. We must all do everything in our power to see that the transfer is accomplished in a thoughtful, constructive manner.

We understand from your attorneys and various other representatives that you would like an opportunity to meet with Juan Miguel Gonzalez. We are prepared to accommodate that request as part of an orderly transfer of the care of Elian to his father.

To that end, please present Elian at Opa-Locka, Fla., where you should proceed to the Main Coast Guard Gate at 2 p.m. Thursday, April 13. Rosa R. Urquiola, a bilingual INS official experienced in immigration matters involving children, will be there to accompany you, Elian, your daughter Marisleysis, and an agreed number of other members of your family to Washington, D.C., for this meeting. Before the meeting, Juan Miguel Gonzalez will have an opportunity to meet privately with his son. During the meeting, Elian will remain with Ms. Urquiola, and INS will have custody and care of Elian during that time. After the meeting, care and parole of Elian will be transferred to Juan Miguel Gonzalez. These successive transfers of parole and care are being ordered pursuant to 8 C.F.R. 212.5,235.2,236.3 (1999).

If you do not wish to meet with Juan Miguel Gonzalez as described above, District Director Bob Wallis and I hereby instruct you to present Elian at the same time and place, i.e., the Main Coast Guard Gate at Opa-Locka Airport, at 2 p.m. on Thursday, April 13. At that time, the parole of Elian into your care will be revoked, and care of Elian will be temporarily transferred to Ms. Urquiola, who will bring Elian to Washington, D.C. Once Elian has arrived in Washington, D.C., he will be paroled into the care of his father. These successive transfers of parole and care are being ordered pursuant to 8 C.F.R. 212,5,235.2,236.3 (1999).

Your and your representatives have frequently stated in the last several weeks that while you did not agree with the Department of Justice's determination in this case or the federal judge's ruling upholding it, you would nevertheless abide by the law. The time has now come to carry through on that commitment, above all for the sake of a boy who deserves to have his reunion with his father take place without any further conflict or stress.

Please contact Mr. Wallis...with your response to this letter.

Sincerely,

Michael A. Pearson
Executive Associate Commissioner for Field Operations

FOR IMMEDIATE RELEASE
AG
THURSDAY, APRIL 13, 2000
(202) 616-2777
WWW.USDOJ.GOV
TODD (202) 514-1888
STATEMENT OF ATTORNEY GENERAL JANET RENO ON
THE ELIAN CASE

Good evening. For the last six weeks, we have worked hard to bring the family together with the hope that the family itself could work out a cooperative agreement. Unfortunately, although still possible, that agreement remains elusive.

An agreement among the family members would by far and away the best solution. It is still a possibility, and we urge all concerned to pursue that possibility. But, it is not in the interest of anyone, least of all Elian, to let his matter drag on.

Commissioner Meissner and I flew to Miami today to do everything possible to resolve this matter in the way least damaging to the child. To this end, we developed a plan in consultation with two child psychiatrists and a child psychologist. Over the past four days these experts met separately with Juan Miguel and Lazaro Gonzalez. Their objective was to determine, no whether, but how best to reunite Elian with his father in the least disruptive manner possible.

They provided us with excellent guidance. And I am very grateful to them.

First, the three experts believe that reunification should take place as soon after the father's arrival in this country, as possible. That is why we asked that Elian be reunited just one week after Mr. Gonzalez arrived here.

Secondly, they feel it would be best if the reunification took place at a neutral location—away from the protesters and cameras. That is why we have secured a neutral retreat site near Washington, D.C. where the family can meet away from the glare of the media, the public and

Cuban government officials.

And third, they believe it would be best for Elian if either Lazaro Gonzalez, his great uncle, or his cousin, Marisleysis, were present. That is why our letter asks that either—or both—of these care givers travel to the retreat site with Elian and be at his side when he is reunited with his father. This will also give the relatives an opportunity to meet privately with Juan Miguel Gonzalez prior to Elian's transfer to his father's care.

We have provided the relatives and Elian the opportunity to travel to the Washington, DC area and meet with Juan Miguel and participate in an orderly transfer. If not, we have provided them alternative instructions that call for them to bring Elian to the Opa-Locka Airport tomorrow afternoon, where his care will be transferred and he will be flown to the Washington area site to be reunited with his father.

I think it is obvious and I believe Mr. Lazaro Gonzalez and his daughter care deeply about Elian. I truly believe that. Since his arrival in the United States they have served as loving caregivers. It is now up to them to ensure that Elian's transition from their care to the care of his father, Juan Miguel Gonzalez, happens in the best and least traumatic way.

As I have said before, this case is about a father and his son. It is a bond that is recognized in the law—and appreciated by every parent around the world. Although Juan Miguel Gonzalez has been separated from his son for four long months, his bond with Elian has never—ever been severed. I know that because I met with Mr. Gonzalez—a man who helped raise Elian and make him into the fine young boy he is today. And without any Cuban officials present, I heard his plea in his own words. He loves his son and he wants him back.

In this last week I have heard so many, reaffirming their faith in the rule of law in this nation. Everyone in this case care deeply about a remarkable 6-year-old boy. A little boy that defines the strength and courage of the human spirit. In the coming days, I urge everyone concerned to think of Elian and to respect the rule of law. Let us make this community a model for what Castro's Cuba is not. Let us make this community a community where people can speak freely without violence and with respect for each other. Let us not disappoint Elian. Let us come together and let us work a way that will best protect the rule of law and this little boy. Thank you.

00-203

FOR IMMEDIATE RELEASE
AG
THURSDAY, APRIL 13, 2000
(202) 616-2777
WWW.USDOJ.GOV
TDD (202) 514-1888
STATEMENT OF ATTORNEY GENERAL JANET RENO

I want to talk to the people of Miami directly today to explain the efforts to resolve the Elian Gonzalez matter and to address the misunderstandings that sometimes exist in a terrible tense situation such as this.

Elian's Miami relatives have asked to meet privately with Juan Miguel Gonzalez, his father, to have the chance to try to convince him that Elian should stay here, and barring that, to at least reassure themselves that he is truly speaking for himself. We have arranged an opportunity for such a meeting—and that opportunity still exists.

As I stated last night in my meeting with Elian's Miami relatives, as well as in our letter to Mr. Lazaro Gonzalez, and in my statement to the press, we have made arrangements for Lazaro Gonzalez and his family to be flown to Washington, DC—at no expense to themselves—to meet with Juan Miguel privately.

This meeting would take place before Elian is transferred to his father's care. It would take place at a private retreat site where this family can finally sit down face-to-face and try to work things out among themselves. If they could work things out amongst themselves, the government would step aside. But if, at the end of the day they could not reach an agreement, the relatives would abide by the rule of law.

We stand by this offer and Juan Miguel Gonzalez has agreed to participate. Unfortunately, Lazaro Gonzalez and his family have refused these arrangements.

Secondly, another rumor that exists is that the government is "federalizing" the streets around Lazaro Gonzalez' home and ejecting the media. These rumors are wrong, flat out wrong. We have not taken any such steps and have no plans to do so. I can also assure the public that they will not see Marshals at 2:01 today attempting to remove the child by force.

I am prepared to enforce the law. But I want to be clear that if we are compelled to enforce our order, we intend to do so in a reasonable, measured way—the approach that we have always taken in this matter. We have the authority to take action, but responsible authority means not only being able to take action—but knowing when and how to take that action.

Finally, the lawyers for Elian's relatives have informed us that they may be filing for a temporary injunction with the 11th Circuit Court of Appeals. Our attorneys will review that motion and respond appropriately in court.

Despite all the tension, it was wonderful to look out the window this morning and to see this beautiful city lying beyond the bay, to look to the west towards the everglades, to look to the Spanish tiles on the roof of the Federal building, to realize that this community represents America and all that it is about. It represents America and the people who have come to this land for freedom, for opportunity, for the right to speak their mind free of violence. It is a great community and a community that if we come together in this time of tension where people obviously disagree with tremendous emotion, but if we come together, if we respect each other, if we respect the rule of law, we can work through it.

00-205

FOR IMMIDIATE RELEASE
AG
WEDNESDAY, APRIL 19, 2000
(202) 616-2777
WWW.USDOJ.GOV
TDD (202) 514-1888
STATEMENT BY ATTORNEY GENERAL JANET RENO
ON THE 11TH CIRCUIT COURT OF APPEALS DECISION

For the past four months, the case of Elian Gonzalez has touched the hearts of virtually every American. It is a case about a 6-year-old boy—and the sacred bond that exists between he and his father. It is that simple—Juan Miguel is in this country and wants his son back.

I believe Elian should be reunited with his father. I have said that all along. The order today from the Court of Appeals says that Elian should not be removed from the country and we will abide by that order. But it does not disagree with my determination that the boy should be reunited with his father in the United States as soon as possible. In fact, the court said that 'we need not decide where or in whose custody Plaintiff should remain while this appeal is pending.'

There are two issues here that must be kept separate. One is whether an asylum application can be brought by distant relatives over the objection of a father who is the sole surviving parent. The other issue is who cares for the child while he is in the United States. The appeal addresses only the asylum issue, not the care issue. The court's order does not preclude me from placing Elian in his father's care while he is in the United States.

The immigration laws clearly call for a child to be placed in the care of a parent in preference to a more distant relative while the child's immigration status is being resolved.

The 11th Circuit's order prevents the child from leaving the country, while the appeal is pending. We will abide by the court's order.

We are still reviewing the court's decision as I have just had a chance to

read it. And we will consider all options and take the course of action most appropriate under the circumstances.
00-220

FOR IMMEDIATE RELEASE
AG
APRIL 21, 2000
(202) 616-2777
WWW.USDOJ.GOV
TDD (202) 514-1888
STATEMENT BY ATTORNEY GENERAL JANET RENO
ON MEETING WITH JUAN MIGUEL GONZALEZ
Attorney General Janet Reno met this afternoon with Juan Miguel Gonzalez. She issued the following statement:

I met this afternoon for the second time with Elian's father, Juan Miguel Gonzalez. He expressed his great concern for the welfare of his son and urged me to take action to reunify him with Elian.

I was deeply moved by Mr. Gonzalez' evident love for his son. I assured him that I would continue working toward the goal of reuniting him with his child, but I also told him that I could not commit to a particular course of action or timetable.

00-223

FOR IMMEDIATE RELEASE
AG
SATURDAY, APRIL 22, 2000
(202) 616-2777
WWW.USDOJ.GOV
TDD (202) 514-1888
ATTORNEY GENERAL STATEMENT REGARDING
THE REMOVAL OF ELIAN GONZALEZ

Good morning. Earlier this morning, federal agents in Miami upheld the rule of law and began to reunite Elian Gonzalez with his father. As I speak, Elian is safe and on a plane headed from Homestead Air Force Base to Andrews Air Force Base where he will be reunited with his father for the first time in 5 months.

When the two are reunited, they will remain together in the United States throughout the appeals process while the injunction is in place. And, in accordance with the Court of Appeals ruling, we will take every step necessary to ensure that Elian does not leave the country while the Court of Appeals injunction is in place.

We have been to great lengths to resolve this case in the least disruptive manner possible. Up until the last [moment], we tried every way we could to encourage Lazaro Gonzalez to voluntarily hand the child over to his father.

Unfortunately, the Miami relatives rejected our efforts—leaving us no other option but the enforcement action.

Elian Gonzalez is a child who needs to be cherished—he needs to have quiet time, private time, to be with his father. And that is what this case is still all about—the bond between father and son. Juan Miguel Gonzalez wants to be with his son and that is what has happened now. More than three months ago the INS determined that only Juan Miguel Gonzalez could speak for his son on immigration matters. From that moment, I could have taken action to return Elian to his father. But I did not.

Instead I gave the Miami relatives a chance to challenge my decision in federal district court. They did and the court sided with the government. It ruled that this was a federal case and that the INS was right to say that the father speaks for the child.

Two weeks ago, a state family court turned away the Miami relatives as well. In a strongly-worded opinion, the judge said not only that the matter belonged in federal court, but that a 6-year-old boy is far too young to make life-altering decisions on his own.

That same week, I traveled to Miami to try to encourage the family members to work out a resolution. The relatives in Miami said all they wanted was a meeting with Juan Miguel Gonzalez, before turning over the child. But when I arranged that meeting, they still refused to produce Elian.

Every step of the way the Miami relatives kept moving the goal posts and raising more hurdles.

That is why I finally directed the relatives to turn over the child 9 days ago. That deadline carried great significance. When Lazaro Gonzalez didn't comply, parole and care was revoked. That means that for the past 9 days, Lazaro Gonzalez has not had lawful custody of Elian.

When the INS places an unaccompanied child into the care of an adult, that adult is required to abide by the directives of the INS. To maintain—as the Miami relatives did—that the INS somehow lacks authority over the immigration parole of a minor in the U.S. simple ignores the law.

So this morning I commenced an operation with the paramount concern being the well-being of Elian and the safety of the agents and others.

After negotiating through the night, I informed the parties that time had run out. At that moment, I gave the go-ahead for the operation.

After I had already set the operation in motion, the intermediaries called back to offer one more counteroffer. I indicated that I was willing to continue to engage in dialogue, but time had run out.

I did until the final moments try to reach a voluntary solution. Law enforcement personnel on the scene, were authorized to, and did, make the final call as to when to enter the Gonzalez home.

Eight agents were in the house during the operation. They were there for three minutes. During that time, a female agent picked up Elian, and spoke to him in Spanish.

The agents then took Elian to Watson Island where they boarded a helicopter bound for Homestead Air Force Base. There he was examined by a doctor to make sure there were no injuries. At that point, he was boarded onto a U.S. Marshal's plane headed to Washington DC where his father is anxiously waiting for his son.

This has been a very emotional case for everyone involved. The most important thing is Elian is safe and that no one is seriously hurt.

As we all await the outcome of the appellate process, I think it is important for us all to accept Elian's long over-due reunion with his father.

It is time to heal the wounds that have divided this community that is so dear to me.

Let us give him and his father the space, the calm and the moral support they need to reconnect and reaffirm their bond between father and son.

00-225

FOR IMMEDIATE RELEASE
AG
SUNDAY, APRIL 23, 2000
(202) 616-2777
WWW.USDOJ.GOV
TDD (202) 514-1888
Media Advisory
Federal Sear Warrant
In Elian Gonzalez Matter

In several news reports earlier today several individuals asserted that the United States law enforcement agents that entered the home of Lazaro Gonzalez did so without a warrant. These statements were incorrect.

The federal agents who went to the house were executing a judicial warrant. The warrant had been obtained from a federal magistrate judge on Friday evening, and gave authority to enter the house, by force it necessary, and recover Elian. The authority to recover Elian was base on rule 41(b)(4) of the Federal Rules of Criminal Procedure. That rule provides warrant authority to recover a person who has been unlawfully restrained. A copy of the judicial warrant is attached.

00-226

FOR IMMEDIATE RELEASE
AG
THURSDAY, June 1, 2000
(202) 514-2007
WWW.USDOJ.GOV
TDD (202) 5140-1888
STATEMENT BY ATTORNEY GENERAL JANET RENO ON THE 11TH CIRCUIT
COURT'S DECISION IN THE ELIAN GONZALEZ CASE

We are pleased that the Court has upheld our decision that only Juan Miguel Gonzalez can speak for his son Elian on federal immigration matters. These three federal appellate judges have now joined with a federal district court judge and a Florida state court judge in recognizing the authority of the INS to make this determination.

This is an important step in achieving the goal we have sought from the very beginning—to give Juan Miguel and his family the opportunity to return to a life together. I am hopeful that this matter will soon reach a final resolution so that Elian, his father and his family, may resume their lives away from the scrutiny of the media and the uncertainty that the legal battle has caused for them.

I hope that all of us—regardless of our disagreements about this case—can join together and wish this family well.

Elian remains in his father's care, but he and his family will not immediately depart the United States. The injunction put in place by the 11th Circuit will remain in effect until the Court's mandate in this case is issued. The INS departure control order put in place on April 22 will remain in place until the injunction is no longer in effect.

Finally, I want to take a moment to commend the dedicated and absolutely splendid attorneys and staff at the Department of Justice and the Immigration and Naturalization Service who have worked so hard over the past six months on this litigation. They, like so many Americans, were moved by this human drama, and they have devoted long hours

to bring about an outcome consistent with the law and our tradition of respect for the parent-child relationship.
00-312

FOR IMMEDIATE RELEASE
AG
FRIDAY, JUNE 23, 2000
(202) 616-2777
WWW.USDOJ.GOV
TDD (202) 514-1888
STATEMENT BY ATTORNEY GENERAL JANET RENO

On the 11th Circuit's Denial of Rehearing in the Elian Gonzalez Case

WASHINGTON, DC—The 11th Circuit Court of Appeals today denied the motion by the Miami relatives of Elian Gonzalez for a rehearing or a rehearing en banc in the case of Elian Gonzalez. Attorney General Janet Reno issued the following statement.

We are pleased that the 11th Circuit Court of Appeals has acted unanimously in denying the motion for rehearing in the case of Elian Gonzalez. Now that the Court has conclusively upheld our decision, I am hopeful that this father and son will soon be able to move on with their lives together.

00-360

FOR IMMEDIATE RELEASE
AG
WEDNESDAY, JUNE 28, 2000
(202) 616-2777
WWW.USDOJ.GOV
TDD (202) 514-1888
STATEMENT BY ATTORNEY GENERAL JANET RENO
ON THE DECISION OF THE SUPREME COURT TO DENY
CERTIORARI IN THE CASE OF ELIAN GONZALEZ
WASHINGTON, DC—The United States Supreme Court today declined to accept for review the case of Elian Gonzalez. The Court's action means that the injunction put in place by the 11th Circuit Court of Appeals will expire at 4:00 PM eastern time today, and Elian Gonzalez will be permitted to depart the U.S. Attorney General Janet Reno issued the following statement:

"I am very pleased that the Supreme Court has declined to review the case of Elian Gonzalez. The law has provided a process, and this little boy now knows that he can remain with his father. All involved have had an opportunity to make their case—all the way to the highest court in the land. I hope that everyone will accept the Supreme Court's decision and join me in wishing this family, and this special little boy, well."

00-373

0-595-23772-X